# The Andrew Carnegie Story

## By Charlie May Simon

ALL MEN ARE BROTHERS: *A Portrait of Albert Schweitzer*
THE ANDREW CARNEGIE STORY
ART IN THE NEW LAND
JOE MASON: *Apprentice to Audubon*
LAYS OF THE NEW LAND
POPO'S MIRACLE
THE ROYAL ROAD
SATURDAY'S CHILD
A SEED SHALL SERVE: *The Story of Toyohiko Kagawa,
 Spiritual Leader of Modern Japan*
THE SUN AND THE BIRCH: *The Story of Crown Prince Akihito
 and Crown Princess Michiko*

# The ANDREW CARNEGIE Story

## by Charlie May Simon

*Illustrated with photographs*

E. P. Dutton & Company, Inc.
*New York*

*To my godchildren*
*Joan Fletcher Terry*
*and*
*John Fletcher Terry*

# Contents

# The Andrew Carnegie Story

# CHAPTER I Dunfermline

Winter had settled in the little town of Dunfermline. All the hills were covered with snow, and the cold east wind blew wet from the North Sea. Like an angry ghost it came howling through the chimneys and over the gabled roofs. The sun, pale and timid, rose late to shine briefly; then the long, weary twilight set in.

In a small one-story cottage on the corner of Moody Street and Priory Lane, young William Carnegie sat at his loom, weaving fine damask for the tables of the rich. His hands moved rhythmically, throwing the shuttle back and forth, with a pause now and then to adjust some break in the thread. He often sang as he worked, his eyes fixed on the slowly growing cloth before him:

> "The king sits in Dunfermline tower
> Drinking the blude-red wine.
> 'O whar will I find a good sailor
> To sail this ship o' mine?'"

His fine tenor voice could be heard, plaintive and somber, above the steady clack and hum of his loom, as he sang

11

one old Scotch ballad after another. His wife, Margaret, spent much of her time these days in the attic bedroom above, with their first-born child. A bonny wee bairn they called him. He was named Andrew after his Grandfather Carnegie, who had danced a jig when he heard the news. But the child, with his chubby face and bright eyes set wide apart, was beginning to show more of a likeness to his mother's father, Thomas Morrison.

The mother's thoughts must often have wandered to the years ahead as she looked down at the baby in her arms. What would the future hold for him? In 1835, a child born of poor parents in Scotland did not have an easy life ahead of him. William Carnegie had taken up the work of his father, a cottage weaver, and his hope was that his son would do the same. But the new steam-powered looms were coming in, competing with the cottage weavers in speed and cheaper prices. One by one the weavers were giving up their hand looms to go to work in mills, at hours set by others and for wages others chose to pay.

Margaret Carnegie dared not hope for fame or riches for her son, but she could at least see to it that he'd grow up with a kind and honest heart. And she would do all in her power to give him a carefree childhood.

> "Late, late yestreen I saw the new moon
> Wi' the auld moon in her arm.
> And I fear, I fear, my dear master,
> That we will come to harm."

Her lullabies were the same ballads her husband sang so well. At eight o'clock the bell from the Abbey tower rang the curfew hour, and the mother whispered to the child some tender message the bells were bringing him. The sound came sweet and clear to his ears, with the wind in the chimney whistling its accompaniment.

These were the sounds the child first knew, the bells of the ancient Abbey, the roar of the wind from the sea, the alternate noises of the loom below, and the songs of old Scotland his parents sang. And his eyes opened first to the warm glow of a lamp and a hearth fire lighting the gloom. He learned to talk in the way of his people. *Andra* he called himself, pronouncing it with the broad *a*, as he heard it. Some words he clipped short, saying *wi'* for *with*, *hae* for *have*, and *fa'* for *fall*. Others were rolled long over the tip of his tongue, and the *world* became the *wurrld*.

Andrew's world grew beyond the little attic living quarters and his father's weaving room below. William Carnegie, determined in his stand against the power looms, moved his family to a larger house in Reid's Park, and added more looms to his shop on the ground floor.

The world outside was, to a child's eyes, immense, and Dunfermline, with its narrow sloping streets and rows of gray stone houses, was its center. The Abbey tower rose like a crown against the sky, with the snow-covered Ochil Hills to the north. Looking south on a clear day from the summit of the hill where the Abbey stood, Andrew could see, beyond the woods and moorland and across the dark waters of the Firth of Forth, the spires of the city of Edinburgh. Sometimes there were excursions to the shores of the Firth of Forth, three miles away, where the waves left treasures of seaweed, shells, and smooth pebbles. Once Andrew's parents took him on the ferry to Edinburgh when the young Queen Victoria came there on a state visit.

South of Edinburgh, hidden behind many a mountain, was England. The land beyond the western ocean was called America, but it was no more than a name to Andrew, the place where his mother's brother and sister had gone. It was now like a half-forgotten dream, that day Aunt Aitken and Uncle William Morrison with his family had come to his parents' home with a map to show where they were going. Niagara, Erie, Pittsburgh: the words sounded strange to his ears.

"You canna remember it, Andra," his mother said with a smile when he spoke of it. "You couldn'a hae been more than two at the time, for it was when we first moved to the house in Reid's Park."

Whether he could remember it or whether he had only heard others talk about it, he could see in his mind the map on rollers, the solemn expression on the faces bending over it, and their excitement when they talked about the new country.

Andrew was the first child in the immediate family on both sides, and the many uncles and aunts spoiled and petted him from the time he was born.

"The bairn's no satisfied wi' one spoon of porridge at a time," said his father's sister Charlotte with an indulgent smile. "He wants two spoons so he'll never be wi'out one in his mouth."

They boasted about how quick and bright he was, how he could memorize a poem and recite it without a mistake. All the clever things he said and did they remembered. There was many a retelling, with laughter, about the time Andrew's father had to carry him on his back when they returned from an excursion at the seashore.

"You're a heavy burden, laddie," the father had said, hoping the boy would offer to get down and walk, for the hill was steep and night was coming on. But Andrew only clung the tighter to his father's neck.

"Ah, Faither, never mind. Patience and perseverance make the man, ye ken," he answered with one of the proverbs he had often heard his father quote.

Margaret Carnegie's sister, the wife of George Lauder, a grocer with a shop on High Street, gave birth to a son, and died a short while afterward. The child was named George, after his father, but to Andrew, who could not pronounce the word, he was *Dod*. The boys grew up together, as close as brothers. "My brother-cousin," Andrew was later to call him. When Andrew was old enough to find his way alone about the streets of Dunfermline, his steps led straight to the shop on High Street. Here, among the sacks of onions and potatoes and barrels of salt herring, he felt he had a second home.

Uncle Lauder had more time for small boys than Andrew's father, and he gave Andrew the love and attention that he gave his own motherless son. *Naig,* he called Andrew, the name little George had given him when he was learning to talk. Naig and Dod. The names were to stay with them throughout their lives.

When Uncle Lauder told the boys stories of Scotland's past, he had a way of making the heroes of old come alive. Robert the Bruce, who had lain buried in Dunfermline Abbey five hundred years and more, was as real to them as their Uncle Bailie Morrison. And William Wallace with his band of sturdy men might have marched this way only yesterday instead of centuries ago. Andrew and his cousin were ready to fight for the good cause all over again. With paper helmets and laths for swords, they made believe they were Bruce and Wallace fighting for Scotland's freedom:

> "Scotts wha' hae wi' Wallace bled,
> Scots whom Bruce hae often led—"

The boys were taught to recite ballads of Scotland's heroes, and poems by Scottish poets, for the amusement of Uncle Lauder's guests.

Sometimes on a winter day, when darkness came all too soon, and it was time for Andrew to go home, his uncle would ask with a teasing smile, "And which way will you go tonight, Naig?"

There were two ways to go from High Street to the Carnegie house at the foot of the hill. One was down the lighted streets by way of the May Gate, and the other was along the deserted graveyard of the old Abbey. To Andrew's mind came the thought, What answer would brave Wallace have made to such a question? Or Robert the Bruce?

"I'll go by way of the Abbey," he always answered.

With his cap on his head and his woolen muffler wrapped around his throat, he whistled as he left his uncle's shop, pretending he was not afraid. But he wished he had not this choice to make. The road led through an arch forming the base of the tower, where the wind blew mournfully. King James, the son of Mary Queen of Scots, once lived in the palace, now in ruins, that adjoined the Abbey, and his son, Charles I, was born here. The story was still told by the old folks about the time the king heard a loud scream from the nurse in the child's room.

"The poor, poor bairn," the nurse was crying. "An old

man came creeping into the room and threw his cloak over the cradle and drew it toward him like he was taking the Prince away."

King James knew, as well as the nurse, that this was the curse of the Devil. Many a tale was told in Scotland about the old man who crept into a room and threw his cloak over a child destined to a life of tragedy.

The moon rose above the old tower and shed its beams on the brown cobbles that paved the street. Andrew whistled louder and hastened his steps until he could see the lighted window of his home. How good it was to step inside, to the smell of mutton broth and oatcakes his mother was cooking!

In the daytime the Abbey was a different place entirely. Often on Sunday afternoons Uncle Lauder took the two boys for a walk around the grounds. With Uncle Lauder, lean and handsome, in a high hat and long brown cape, swinging his briarwood cane, he could feel safe anywhere. They passed the ruins of the old palace, and the uncle told about the kings who had once lived there. All that was left now was the long wall with the royal kitchen between the gardens and the Abbey.

They came to a place that overlooked Pittencrieff Glen, bordering the Abbey grounds. It was gray and mysterious from where they stood, like some vision seen through a mist. When Andrew heard the word Paradise, this is the picture that came to his mind. The Queen might have her Windsor Castle, but Lord Hunt, who owned Pittencrieff Glen, was more to be envied. Andrew could hear the song of the lark and thrush as they flitted through the trees, and the rustle of the grass where a hare or perhaps a deer was passing. The sainted Queen Margaret was buried somewhere in this glen, and on a rocky point rising above the rivulet was a grass-grown stump of stones that had once been a tower. Here the king of the old song sat drinking his blood-red wine, calling for a good sailor to sail his ship in a storm.

Andrew could never pass this place without trying to catch a glimpse of the inside, whether over a wall, through a lodge gate, or under the iron grille above the stream, wishing with all his heart he could see it closer.

"Even if others were allowed there, the laird would never let Morrison kin set foot in the glen, you can be sure of that," Uncle Lauder said.

Andrew and George, both Morrison kin on their mother's side, nodded solemnly, for they understood. Lord Hunt had once owned the Abbey and palace also, and they too had been closed to the public. It was Grandfather Morrison who, with a group of followers, demanded the rights of the people to enter there. Later his oldest son, Thomas, known now as Uncle Bailie to the boys, took up the demand. He was the leader of a band of men who tore down a certain wall. This brought about his arrest, but he and the citizens won a victory in the highest court. The Abbey and the Palace were open to everybody from then on in spite of the wishes of Lord Hunt. The lord could keep the gates of the Glen closed, and he did, with orders that none could enter without his permission, and especially no kin of the Morrisons.

Dunfermline was still a town of patriotic men who cared as much for freedom as any of the heroes of old. Wearing their weaver aprons, they gathered on street corners after the noon meal, or at one church or another in the evening, to talk about political affairs. They rebelled against the privileges of aristocracy, and against the unfair laws these people forced upon them.

"Death to privilege!" Andrew shouted, taking up the cry of the older men.

He had no idea what was meant by privilege, but his father knew, and was against it, and that was enough for him. He was never happier than when he was allowed to go to the meetings, where he listened wide-eyed while his father or one of the uncles spoke.

Uncle Lauder often took part in the meetings, but it was the fiery, high-pitched voice of Uncle Thomas Morrison that was most often heard. He read editorials from the liberal London papers aloud to the men, and he shouted his arguments for human rights, thumping his knotted briarwood cane for emphasis. There was talk of America. It was a country so new that there were men still living who remembered when the colonies became an independent nation. Why couldn't the same be done for Scotland?

One night Andrew was awakened by a tap at the window, and he heard a voice whispering to his parents. Thomas Morrison had been arrested. He had defied authorities by holding a meeting a few miles out of town. The sheriff and the Queen's soldiers had gone out to make the arrest and had brought him back to Dunfermline. They were followed by a group of angry men, muttering to themselves that they would storm the jail, if necessary, to rescue their leader.

Thomas Morrison, radical though he was, believed in order. He stood at a window of the room where he was held and spoke to the crowd gathered in the street below.

"If there is a friend of the good cause among you, let him fold his arms."

The muttering stopped, and every man stood with folded arms.

"Now depart in peace," Thomas Morrison said, and the men walked quietly away.

The government authorities wisely dismissed the charges against him. He became a popular hero, and soon after this event he was elected to the town council. Later he became the bailiff and was known from then on as Bailie Morrison.

About the time of Thomas Morrison's troubles with the authorities, the Carnegies moved back to Moody Street. The larger house in Reid Park, with the new looms, had been a mistake. William Carnegie found it harder than ever to make a living for his family. Orders for table linen were going more and more to the mills, and the cottage looms stood idle for long periods at a time. Andrew saw the look of anxiety on his mother's face each time the father went off to the dealers who furnished the web to be woven into the finished cloth. He also saw the despair of both when his father came back empty-handed.

Margaret Carnegie, a true Morrison, was a strong, determined woman. She was not one to stand idly by while her family was in want. The house on Moody Street had room enough for her to open a small grocery shop. Since they were not far from the Rolland Street school, she added a shelf of sweets to sell to the children, who called her place the sweetie shop.

Andrew was old enough by then to do small chores for his mother. He ran errands and made deliveries to near-by houses, and he brought water from the public well at the head of the street. He dreamed of the things he'd do when he grew to be a man. He would earn enough money, just how, he did not know, to give his parents a life of ease. There would be no worries over idle looms then, and no more long hours of work in a shop. There might even be a big house on one of the fashionable streets. Oh, he could soar high in his dreams! Some day he'd buy them a carriage to ride in, and his mother would wear dresses of silk. There was a song his father often sang:

> "When Alack, Jock and Jeannettie
> Are up and got their lair,
> They'll serve to gar the boatie row,
> And lighten a' our care."

But Alack, Jock and Jeannettie of the song had to grow up first, and get their lore, or education, before they could lighten their parents' care. Andrew had uneasy thoughts about Mr. Martin's school on Rolland Street. He was almost eight, and all the boys of the neighborhood who were his age were already in school, but he stubbornly refused to go. Uncle Lauder could teach him all he needed to know. Couldn't he recite long poems of Burns and Scott? And didn't he know the history of Scotland as well as any schoolboy? He knew English history also. Uncle Lauder had a way of teaching so he'd never forget what he learned. He pictured the monarchs of England, each in a certain place over the walls of the room. In his mind Andrew could see King John on the mantelpiece signing the Magna Charta. Queen Victoria was on the door with the infant Prince of Wales. And of course there was Oliver Cromwell, worth all of them put together, so Uncle Lauder said.

"I made myself a boy so the boys could become men," Uncle Lauder was afterward to say of this period.

Andrew's parents had once indulgently promised him they would not send him to school until he asked to go. They were sure that when the time came, and he saw his playmates start, he would want to join them; but as far as Andrew was concerned, he had no intention of doing so. He held them to their promise. An honest person's word is never broken. The elder Carnegies, however, had their own way of solving the problem. They had a talk with Robert Martin, the teacher. A few days later the young man invited Andrew, with some of his playmates among the pupils, to go on an outing.

They hiked along country lanes bordered by hedgerows, and they ate their lunch beside a running burn, or brook. The hillsides were gold with broom, and farther up the slopes the purple heather was in bloom. Bumblebees darted in and out of the creamy hedgethorn blossoms, and the meadow larks and curlews made the day gay with their song.

Andrew returned home in the evening tired but happy. It had been fun. Perhaps he was missing something after all by staying out of school. His parents must have exchanged a knowing smile, for they were not in the least surprised to hear him say he'd like to start to school now.

Robert Martin was a born teacher. He was strict, as teachers were at that time, punishing without hesitation a boy who misbehaved or came to class without knowing his lesson. "Ye hae not been put into this world to enjoy yourselves, but to do your duty," he often said to the children. But he could make the lessons as interesting as Uncle Lauder had done.

Andrew wondered why he had once so dreaded school.

He was impatient now with anything that kept him away or made him late. He hurried through his morning chores so he could be on his way. Never did the water trickle so slowly as when he took his pitcher to the public well, with the schoolbell soon to ring. A group of housewives, muffled up in plaid shawls, stood gossiping in the line ahead of him, with no thought of a waiting schoolboy. Some of them came late and tried to push their way up front where they had left old cans the night before, to mark their place. When Andrew refused to make room for them, they clucked their tongues in disapproval.

"He's an awfu' laddie," they said.

It mattered little to Andrew then what they thought of him. He rushed back to the house, with the water splashing in the pitcher, then hurried on his way. The walk to school took about five minutes, just long enough to learn from memory two double verses of the Psalms that each of the pupils had to recite. He read words such as "They that go down to the sea in ships, that do business in the great waters. These see the works of the Lord and the wonders of the deep." He closed the book and repeated the words over to himself until he could say them without faltering.

His cheeks still burned with embarrassment when he remembered his first week in school. He had taken his place with the other pupils, standing in a semicircle, with toes touching the chalk line. As the names were called, each pupil answered with one of the Proverbs. Andrew, at the foot of the line, listened as they chanted, "A good name is rather to be chosen than great riches, and loving favor rather than silver and gold." Or "A man that hath friends must show himself friendly: and there is a friend that sticketh closer than a brother." He racked his brains. His parents were always quoting proverbs. "Patience and perseverance make the man," "Nothing is a man's truly, but what he comes by duly—" Somehow they didn't sound the same as the ones the other pupils were quoting.

"Andra Carnegie," Mr. Martin called.

Andrew blurted out, "Take care of your pence and the pounds will take of themselves."

His mother had many an occasion to use these words, but never had they been followed by such an uproar of laughter as now.

"This proverb of Benjamin Franklin is no doubt a good one, lad," the teacher said, trying to hide his smile. "But it is scarcely in keeping with the sacred Proverbs of Solomon. Go to your Bible for tomorrow's quotation."

One day an older boy told Andrew that England was larger than Scotland. It couldn't be true, he thought. Surely the boy was only teasing. Uncle Lauder would know. He'd find out the truth from him.

"Not at all, Naig," Uncle Lauder said when he asked him. "If Scotland were rolled out as England is, Scotland would be larger. But you wouldn't want the Highlands rolled down, would you?"

Again, when Andrew was told that England had a larger population than Scotland, Uncle Lauder had an answer for that also.

"Aye, Naig, seven to one. But there were more odds than that against us at Bannockburn, ye ken."

It hadn't mattered to brave Robert the Bruce how many Englishmen came marching against him at Bannockburn.

Hadn't the arrows of his men sent them in retreat all the way to the English border!

Andrew was small for his age, but wiry and strong. He had a happy disposition, and from the beginning he made friends easily. The school grounds were lively at recess with races run and mock battles fought. The boys of Andrew's age looked to him as their leader. On Saturday holidays they went with him to the fields outside town to gather clover and dandelions for his pet rabbits. To have one named after them was reward enough.

Another child was born to the Carnegies soon after Andrew started to school. His hair was as light as the flax his father wove, and he had his mother's sparkling black eyes. They named him Tom after Grandfather Morrison.

Margaret Carnegie saw that her sons did not suffer because of their poverty. She cooked nourishing meals for them, mutton broth, oatcakes or barley-meal porridge. She made their clothes and kept them washed and mended, and on Saturday nights they had a tub bath before the fire. It was not until Andrew was old enough to help keep the shop's accounts that he knew how little his parents had to live on. Sometimes his dreams of a fine house and a carriage faded, and he thought only of enough to live on day by day.

He earned his first penny, one his teacher gave him, for reciting a long poem by Robert Burns, "Man Was Made to Mourn."

There were seven long stanzas, and he recited them to the end without a mistake. It was the kind of poem Uncle Lauder liked to teach him, one that told of man's injustice to man:

"See yonder poor, o'erlabour'd wight,
So abject, mean, and vile,
Who begs a brother of the earth
To give him leave to toil."

Andrew thought of his father. Certainly there was nothing abject, mean and vile about William Carnegie, but, like the man in the poem, he went out day after day, asking only leave to toil. He was down to his last loom. One by one the others had been sold, but they were worth little more than the wood they were made of. The hungry forties, this period was called, when the Industrial Revolution was throwing so many men out of work. The time had come when the Carnegies knew things could not go on any longer as they were. When the father came home one day from delivering some damask cloth to the dealer, and said simply, "I have no more work," the whole family wept together. Andrew, at eleven began to feel the terrible burden of responsibility.

Another relative of the mother had gone to America, a sister with her husband, Andrew Hogan, and his brother. Glowing letters had come from them and from Uncle William and Aunt Aitken, telling of life there.

"This country is far better for the working man than the old one, and there is room enough and to spare, notwithstanding the thousands that flock to her borders every year."

"We will go there too," Margaret Carnegie said, for she was the one who made the decisions for the family.

Her husband agreed. "It's not of myself I am thinking," he said quietly. "I want to go where our sons will have a better opportunity than they'd find here."

Once the move was decided upon, they set about making preparations. Their problem was raising enough money to take them there. The household furniture was put up for auction, but it did not bring them enough to pay for the passage. If William Carnegie despaired, his wife was not ready to give up. She turned to a friend of her childhood, Ella Ferguson Henderson, or Ailie Fargie, as they called her. She offered them twenty pounds, money she and her husband had been saving to buy a home of their own. Uncle Bailie objected to the move, sure it would end in failure, but he and Uncle Lauder signed a note guaranteeing the money would be paid back.

Uncle Lauder managed all the details of buying tickets, making reservations, and studying schedules. Andrew went for a last Sunday-afternoon stroll with him and Dod around the Abbey grounds. The Abbey was never so beautiful to him. He took a farewell look at the five recessed arches of the doorway, carved in stone, and the splendid nave inside, with lofty columns built during the time of William the Conqueror. Seven kings lay buried there. Sir Walter Scott, who had died two years before Andrew was born, had loved the old Abbey. The elder Carnegies had once seen him there making a sketch of it, when he visited Dunfermline. Then there was one last glimpse through the lodge gate of Pittencrieff Glen.

The time came to say goodbye to the teacher and the classmates at school. Four years had passed since Andrew started there. It was his first and it was to be the last school he'd ever attend.

In the days that followed, Andrew was caught up in the excitement of packing and getting ready to go on the long, adventurous journey. He had never seen his father so cheerful. It was as if a heavy load had dropped from his shoulders.

When he sang, it was not of Scotland, but of the new world they would soon see:

> "To the West, to the West, to the land of the free;
> Where the mighty Missouri rolls down to the sea;
> Where a man is a man, even though he must toil,
> And the poorest may gather the fruits of the soil."

Uncle Bailie, Uncle Lauder, and Dod went with them on the omnibus that ran on the coal railroad. Andrew stood looking out the window and saw the town of Dunfermline fade slowly in the distance until all that was left was the noble Abbey on the summit of the hill. That too disappeared, but in his mind he could still see the huge block letters of the balustrade of the tower, spelling the words KING ROBERT THE BRUCE. It was only now that he realized what it meant to leave this place he loved. He was saying goodbye, perhaps forever. Never again would he hear the sweet bells of the tower ringing the curfew hour. So many times, when he was small, he had raced to get into bed before the last chimes sounded. He had thought then that the bells were ringing messages to him. Had he been up to some mischief during the day? Or had he been obedient and good?

It was May, the time of nesting birds with songs as sweet as the sound of the bells. The snow had melted from the low hills, and the slopes were like a woven cloth of brown and green and gold. Wild flowers bloomed along the roadside, primroses, forget-me-nots and thyme. Scotland was beautiful to Andrew then.

When they reached the Firth of Forth, they were rowed across in a small boat to the Edinburgh steamer on the other side. Uncle Lauder stood at the stern behind Andrew. He had been telling him about the country that was to be his new home. There was room for a boy to get ahead there, he said, and Andra was the kind of lad who would go far. The time came to say goodbye. Uncle Lauder put a sovereign in Andrew's hand, and said, "Now, Naig, go." Andrew started on two or three seats forward. Suddenly it was more than he could bear. He turned back and threw his arms around his uncle.

"I canna leave ye! I canna leave ye!" he cried.

Passengers stood at the side of the waiting steamer, looking on, and the captain called down from the top of the paddle-wheel box that he couldn't wait any longer.

"Come, lad," one of the sailors said, and Andrew felt himself lifted up on deck, to be carried away from all that was dear and familiar.

## CHAPTER II   Bobbin Boy

There was still another farewell to Scotland and one more ship to board, a large sailing ship called the *Wiscasset,* anchored at the Glasgow port. Andrew was caught up in the gaiety and excitement of the other passengers when at last, after a long and tiresome wait, the anchor was up, the sails set, and the pilot stood at the wheel, guiding the ship out to the open sea. Boxes, chests, and bedding had long been put in place; and passengers, who had been strangers until then, met on deck, smiling and talking as if they were old friends. As the ship sailed on, they stood watching the land grow smaller and smaller.

A quiet mood came over the passengers then. Andrew was not alone in his thoughts of home. Many were leaving never to return. Some were going in search of freedom, some were driven away because of ideals and beliefs, and some wanted an opportunity the Old World could not give them. But somewhere beyond that dark thin line on the horizon, there was a place dear to each of them.

In Scotland there was scarcely a stream or bank or slope

of hill that did not have its heart-stirring song. Among the passengers from Scotland there were thoughts of the bonnie, bonnie banks of Loch Lomond, the braes of Yarrow, the banks and braes of Bonnie Doon, and Maxwelltown's banks that were bonnie too. And of course there was the tower of Dunfermline.

The first steamship had crossed the Atlantic ten years earlier, making the voyage in thirteen and a half days, but the sailing vessel *Wiscasset* was seven weeks at sea. It was long enough to give a boy of twelve a sense of loyalty to it, looking upon it as a home between two places. He shared the sailors' pride when they sailed merrily along in fair wind and fine weather, making eleven knots an hour. When they passed another ship and the *Wiscasset*'s colors were hoisted, he could feel they were his colors too. He listened eagerly as the captains called out through their speaking trumpets, exchanging latitude and longitude, and telling where they were from and where bound.

The sailors, strong men with bronzed, weather-beaten faces and tattooed arms and chests, became his friends. He followed them as they went about their work. He walked as they did, with a swinging, rolling gait, and he learned from them the language of the sea.

The sailors showed Andrew how to tie the sailor's knots: the reef knot, the sheet bend, the marline spike hitch. He learned the names of all the sails, from the foremast jib sail to the spanker at the stern. On Sundays, when they had plum duff as a special treat, he was invited to share the meal with them.

For a boy whose horizons had been bound on all sides by high hills and mountain peaks, the sky must have seemed immense. He saw the sun come up from the sea in the early morning, and he saw it go back down when it had run its course. Sometimes, on a clear night, the stars were so sharp and bright it was as though he could reach up and gather them in his hands like sparkling toys.

To the older passengers, crowded uncomfortably in their quarters, the days dragged endlessly, prolonging the terrible suspense of what lay ahead at the journey's end. Some lay sick on their bedding, some sat on chests or packing boxes, and some paced the deck, looking out on the boundless stretch of water. The moods of the sea had given them some foretaste of the destiny waiting for them in the New World. There would be storms to brave, and enforced idleness, and there would also be times of smooth sailing.

Slowly on the western horizon a thin blue strip emerged and gradually grew larger, seeming to come toward them. At last they heard a rolling, hollow sound like distant thunder. It was the pounding of the surf, the sailors said. Dark and light spots of woods and fields began to show, then single trees stood out, and houses and farms and towns could be seen.

The passengers bathed from buckets of sea water, and put on the best clothes they owned. When they came out on deck they stood looking intently at the land. Their faces showed mingled emotions of hope, dread, and doubt, and sadness, too, at thought of the home they had left behind.

The pilot ship came to meet them, and the *Wiscasset* was guided through New York Harbor. The sailors ran up the rigging, as graceful as cats, too busy for a last goodbye to Andrew. The sails were furled; the anchor was dropped; and the long voyage was over.

There were few on board who had not some friend or relative to meet them and take them in until they could start out on their own. A cottage weaver named Sloane, from Dunfermline, with his wife, who had been a girlhood friend of Margaret's, and three sons, shared their small home with the Carnegies. They stayed there only long enough for William Carnegie to make arrangements to take his family by canal to Pittsburgh, where the relatives were waiting for them.

Andrew's brain was in a whirl of new impressions. America came to mean many things to him. It was at first a busy city with streets sunnier and wider than the streets of Dunfermline, where cabs and coaches and carriages passed up and down, with now and then a farmer's wagon bringing produce to town. America meant the excitement of jostling crowds, and it meant one man's kindness to a bewildered boy. The *Wiscasset* was still in port, a link to the old home across the ocean. On a hot July day Andrew was walking on the grounds of the old fort at the battery called Castle Garden. He saw one of the sailors from the ship, Robert Barryman, dressed in his shore clothes, blue middy jacket, white trousers, and a hat with streamers perched jauntily on his head. Surely there was no one handsomer in all New York than Robert Barryman the sailor, Andrew thought. The man gave a shout of greeting when he recognized the young passenger from his ship.

"Come, lad, we'll have something to quench our thirst," he said.

He led the way to a refreshment stand and ordered sarsaparilla. Andrew watched in fascination as an old woman filled two glasses from a highly ornamented brass vessel. The delicious taste of the cool drink and the kindness of the sailor who bought it for him were to linger long in his memory.

The journey to Pittsburgh lasted three weeks, and for Andrew it was a long and happy holiday. They floated on the canal by day, pulled by strong horses on the towpath, and at night they slept on narrow bunks built like bookshelves, one above the other against the wall. Scotland was far away now.

America became a place of great distances, of lonesome cabins surrounded by dense forests, of scattered towns, with now and then a thriving new city built on a river bluff. The Carnegies stayed all night on the wharf boat at Beaver, waiting for the steamboat to take them up the Ohio to Pittsburgh. There the mosquitoes stung them until their faces were so swollen they could scarcely see, but this did not keep Andrew from sleeping through it all.

Finally they reached Allegheny City across the river from Pittsburgh. Now America meant home. The Morrisons and the Hogans were waiting with a warm welcome for the weary travelers. To Andrew's ears there came again the familiar speech of Scotland. From then on, he was to be divided all his life in his loyalty between the country of his birth and the country that welcomed him.

"Yes, I'm Scotch, and I'm proud of it," he said when some boys laughed at his accent.

There were hills on the horizon, and steep, sloping streets in Pittsburgh as at Dunfermline. But in Dunfermline the streets were ancient, worn smooth by the tramping of many feet, and the houses, somber and strong, had been built to last forever. Here there was a raw newness. The streets were muddy, and hogs roamed up and down as scavengers. Vacant lots between the red-painted houses were turned into cabbage patches. There was still talk about the great fire of 1845, three years ago. It had been fanned from a washerwoman's outdoor fire, built under a pot of clothes, and in five hours it had swept over twenty square blocks, burning down more than a thousand houses and destroying the entire business part of the city.

The relatives lived on Rebecca Street, a poor section close to the waterfront of Allegheny City. Uncle Hogan's brother had built a weaving shop on the back of the lot owned by Aunt Aitken. It had a second story of two rooms where the Carnegie family could live, rent free. Here William Carnegie took up weaving tablecloths again.

His songs of hope began to die. There were no dealers here to furnish web for cloth to be woven on order, as there had once been at Dunfermline. The only way to sell the handwoven linen was to peddle it from door to door. The quiet William Carnegie was a weaver and not a salesman. The competition from the mills, with their cheaper machine-made cloth, was greater here than in Scotland. In the new country, as in the old, he had to beg leave to toil.

At thirteen Andrew again felt a heavy sense of responsibility. If he could only find a job, any kind of job, to add his wages to the little his father could earn. If between them they could make as much as $25 a month, he thought, they could live well without being dependent on others as they were now. U. S. 1457363

Once more Margaret Carnegie decided that, since something must be done, it was up to her to do it. Keeping a grocery shop was out of the question. Even the smallest one would take more money than they could possibly scrape up; besides, she had no experience in buying and selling in this new country. Whatever work she did must be in her own home, where she could look after her family, prepare their meals, keep their clothes clean and mended, and the house tidy.

Thomas Morrison, her father, had been a master shoemaker in Dunfermline. He had taught his sons his trade, and he had also taught his daughters to bind shoes. "Hand-i-cation" was as important as "head-i-cation," he had said. Margaret Carnegie now went to Mr. Phipps, the neighborhood shoemaker, and asked for work. He gave her shoes to bind in her own home and paid her $4 a week for the work. Often at midnight, long after her husband and sons were asleep, she was still sitting at her sewing, to earn the needed extra money.

"What about Andra?" the aunts and uncles asked. "Hasn't he found a job yet?"

Even the five-year-old Tom was of some help. He sat beside his mother during the day, waxing thread and threading needles for her, while she told him stories and sang songs of old Scotland, as she had done when Andrew was that age.

"Andra's a likely lad, and quick to learn," the brother of Uncle Hogan said one day. "If a basket of knickknacks could be fitted out for him, he could make a good little sum of money peddling them around the wharfs."

Margaret Carnegie had seen something of wharf life, the drunken, brawling men and the slovenly women, during the three-week journey by canal from New York to Pittsburgh. Her dark eyes blazed with anger as she threw down her sewing and sprang to her feet.

"What! My son a peddler, mixing with those rough men on the wharfs!" she cried, shaking a finger in the bewildered man's face. "I'd rather see him thrown in the Allegheny River. Now leave me!"

When the well-meaning Mr. Hogan had gone, she sat down and cried. Then, wiping her eyes with the corner of her apron, she put her arms around her two sons.

"You mustn't mind my foolishness," she said. "There are many things you boys can do in this world. Just remember always to do what is right, and you'll grow up to be useful men, honored and respected."

The father finally found a job that winter, in a cotton mill owned by a fellow Scotsman. Andrew, too, was given work as a bobbin boy. Each weekday they started out together before dawn, and returned home twelve hours later, after dark, without having had a glimpse of the sun all day. The hours dragged, and the work of winding bobbins was dull and monotonous enough to stifle the least of dreams. But at the end of the sixth day, when Andrew brought home his weekly pay, he was filled with pride. He was a breadwinner now. Instead of being dependent on his parents, he was doing his part in contributing to the support of the family.

The first job led to another, this time in a bobbin factory. Andrew was put to work running a small steam engine and firing the boiler in the cellar. He was paid $2.00 a week, $0.80 more than he had been earning, but the work was more trying than winding bobbins at the cotton mill. If the gauges were too low, the workers complained that they were not getting enough power, and if they were too high the boilers could explode. The steam gauges haunted him even in his dreams. Many a night he woke up from a nightmare of gauges all about him, some with pressure too high and some too low. During the day, back at his work in the darkness of the cellar, grimy with coal dust, the game of his childhood kept him going. What would Robert the Bruce have done? Or the brave Wallace? Would they give up? Never! Nor would any true Scotsman.

John Hay, the owner of the factory, was also a Scot. He took a liking to this energetic young boy with the broad accent of his own country.

"What kind of hand do you write, lad?" he asked one day.

He gave Andrew some writing to do, then looked it over, nodding with satisfaction. He had no clerk, and since his own handwriting was poor, he took Andrew away from the steam engine in the cellar and gave him the work of making out bills. Later, when he saw the boy was good at figures, he allowed him to keep the accounts as well. The books were kept in single entry, and Andrew, with the experience he had had keeping accounts for his mother's shop in Dunfermline, could handle this as well as an older clerk.

America at that time was the right place for a boy with dreams, and with energy and adventurous spirit enough to make those dreams come true. The country was growing the way a boy grows, robust, boisterous, awkward perhaps, but with supreme assurance. By 1849 the original thirteen colonies had grown to thirty states, with territories reaching all the way to the Pacific Coast. There was still a restless movement to the West, as there had been since the country was first settled. Men set out alone on horseback or afoot, or they went with their families in groups, by boat or covered wagon.

William Carnegie followed with interest a bill before

Congress, granting 160 acres of homestead land to any man who had no other land, and who was willing to cultivate and live on it.

"Be sure and write your Uncle Lauder about it, for it's the greatest reform of the age," he said to Andrew.

"Send out your poor, tax-ridden honest men and they will soon get a home here," Andrew added in his letter.

Perhaps the father had dreams of joining the trek to the West and creating a home for his family, but the little two-room house with the weaving shop on Rebecca Street was as far west as the Carnegies were to go. The frontiers for Andrew to explore were of another kind. He saw the first telegraph line stretched into Pittsburgh from the east, and soon another line was added to the west. Steam packets began bringing mail to and from Cincinnati. There was talk of some day building a railroad from Philadelphia over the Allegheny Mountains into Pittsburgh, but men without vision laughed at a scheme so wild and impossible.

For Andrew, nothing seemed impossible. At his work in the bobbin factory he kept his sight on the step ahead, though it was not always easy to do so. One of his duties, in addition to the clerical work, was to bathe the newly made bobbins in vats of crude petroleum, or rock oil, from the Tarentum salt well. In the small separate room where the vats were kept, the smell of oil was so vile that even a Wallace or a Bruce would have turned pale. Whether in here, or perched on his high bookkeeper's stool, Andrew knew that life held more than this for him. Once, back in Dunfermline, when he was a small child sitting in church with his father, he had his first awareness of beauty. He was trying to listen to the long, dull sermon when his eyes were drawn to the end window behind the pulpit. All the other windows of the church were of poor plain glass, but this one was bordered with small squares of red and blue glass. He had seen it many times before, but, with the light filtering through the colors, it was as if this were the first time, and the beauty of it filled his eyes and heart and mind. The memory of this experience came often to him, and he knew that the world had glorious things to offer. He knew, too, that if they were to be his, it would be only through his own effort.

He learned that the larger business firms were keeping their books in double entry, and he decided to study it. He persuaded three of the boys in his neighborhood to join him, and every night they crossed the bridge to Pittsburgh to take a course in this newer method of bookkeeping.

One evening he returned home to hear from his parents that Uncle Hogan had told them of an opening for a messenger boy at the telegraph office. The manager, David Brooks, had spoken of it when the two were playing checkers the night before.

"Do you know where I can find a good boy?" Mr. Brooks had asked.

"My wife has a nephew who might do," Uncle Hogan had replied. "I'll find out if he wants the job."

Did Andrew want it! He knew how a bird in a cage must feel when it found the door left open. He could scarcely wait for morning so he could rush out and apply. His mother was as happy as he was, but his father had his doubts. There was a Scotch proverb, often quoted, "Who never climbs will never fa'." The wage offered was $2.50 a week.

"For that much money they'll want an older boy," he said. Andrew was then fourteen, but small for his age, and looked younger. "There'll be messages to be delivered late at night sometimes, out beyond the city where it's dangerous for a boy to go."

He felt that Andrew should let well enough alone and stay with the job he had, but his wife did not agree. She had her way, and the father consented to allow the boy at least to apply for the job. Andrew knew, though nothing was said about it, that his father went secretly to John Hay for advice. Hay was interested in the boy's welfare, and promised the elder Carnegie that if things did not turn out well for Andrew at the telegraph office, he could always come back to the bobbin factory.

"I'll go along with you, Andra," William Carnegie said.

Together they walked the two miles from Allegheny to Pittsburgh across the river. Andrew had dressed with care, wearing his only white linen shirt, which his mother had washed and ironed, and his short, tight jacket of blue, which he called a roundabout. When they reached the telegraph office on the corner of Fourth and Wood streets, Andrew pleaded with his father to wait outside and let him go in alone for the interview. Mr. Brooks's office was on the second floor, and as he climbed the stairs alone, Andrew felt his confidence come back to him.

"I haven't had any experience," he admitted in the interview.

Thinking, perhaps, of his father waiting on the street corner, pacing up and down in his anxiety, Andrew went on to tell why he might not be suitable for the job. He lived across the river in Allegheny and didn't know the streets of Pittsburgh very well. Perhaps, too, he wasn't large enough or strong enough. Perhaps he wouldn't do.

"But all I ask is a chance," he burst out.

"How soon can you start?" Mr. Brooks asked.

"I can start right now," Andrew answered without hesitation.

Mr. Brooks called to his other messenger boy.

"This is Andrew Carnegie," he said. "Take him out with you and let him see how the work is done."

Andrew found a chance to go outside where his father waited, to give him the good news that he had already started to work. Whatever doubts William Carnegie may have had when he turned back home, there were none in Andrew's mind. He had a foot on the ladder now, and he was ready to climb. There would be fifty cents more a week to bring home, but that was not all. He had come out of the dark factory, streaked with coal dust and reeking with the smell of oil. Now he was in the light, in the sunshine and fresh air.

One thing that worried him was finding his way about the streets of Pittsburgh to deliver messages. He set himself the task of learning the names of the streets, and the buildings on each one. Beginning with the corner where the telegraph office stood, he studied the signs of all the business houses, repeating them over and over to himself to keep them in his memory. One day it was Wood Street, another it was Fourth; then he went to the streets beyond, up one side and down the other. The streets of Pittsburgh, instead of the steam gauges, now haunted his dreams, and every night before drifting off to sleep he whispered to himself the names of business firms in their proper order, on Market Street, on Water Street, on Smithfield Street.

He was not long in recognizing the men who most often received messages. There were General Robinson who had been the first white child born west of the Ohio, Judge Wilkins, Edwin M. Stanton. The list grew, and when he met them on the street he was able to save them time by giving them the message then and there.

Sometimes a message took him beyond the lighted streets of the business district, past vacant lots and cabbage patches, to some private home. There anxious eyes looked out from behind curtains as he approached, for no telegraphic messages ever came this way except to bring news of sickness or death. Ten words could hold a world of sadness and grief.

The older messenger boy was promoted, and David Mc-Cargo, whose parents had come from Scotland, was hired to take his place. The telegraphic business was growing so fast that soon another boy was needed.

"Do you know anyone suitable for the job?" Andrew was asked.

He thought of his friend Robert Pitcairn, one of the boys in his neighborhood who, like himself, had been born in Scotland. Andy, Bob, and Davy, the three Scots boys called themselves. They took turns, two at a time, staying late to deliver night messages, or arriving early in the morning to sweep the office floors.

When James Reid, the general superintendent, came to the Pittsburgh office, the messenger boys were called in for an inspection. Everything was in order except one thing. The boys would look better in uniform, he thought, so he sent them to a tailor to be measured for jackets and knickers of dark green cloth. At this time not even policemen or firemen wore uniforms. Andrew, especially, was delighted with the new clothes, and at his suggestion the boys called on Mr. Reid to thank him.

This was a happy period in Andrew Carnegie's life. Colonel Glass, the manager of the downstairs office, gave the boys, in turn, the messages to deliver as they came in from the operating room above. On the second of November, three weeks before Andrew's fourteenth birthday, he saw his name in print for the first time, in the Pittsburgh *Gazette*.

"A messenger boy by the name of Andrew Carnegie employed by the O'Reilly Telegraph Company found a draft for the amount of five hundred dollars yesterday. Like an honest little fellow, he promptly made known the fact and deposited the paper in good hands, where it waits identification."

No doubt this statement was read over again many times by the proud parents, and clipped out to be sent to the relatives in Scotland.

Sometimes there were rewards for messages delivered promptly, a pocketful of apples from a wholesale fruitstore, sweet cakes from a baker, candy from a confectioner's shop. Best of all there was the Pittsburgh Theater, where a boy, delivering a message while a performance was on, was allowed to see it from the top gallery. Andrew had never been inside a theater or a concert hall until then. He looked on in fascination as the green curtains parted upon an enchanted world of make-believe. Villains plotted, heroines suffered, and brave heroes made everything right again.

There were minstrel shows also. Men with blackened faces paraded around the stage in a song-and-dance act, with banjoes playing and tambourines jingling. They did the cakewalk and they strutted, and they sat in a semicircle with the interlocutor in the middle and Mr. Bones and Sambo on the two ends, telling minstrel jokes. The three boys exchanged duties so that each one could have a chance to see a show. Jenny Lind came to Pittsburgh, and Andrew heard her sing.

"When I heard her," he wrote to Dod, "I thought Oh if she would only sing some Scotch songs, if she would give us 'Auld Lang Syne' I would have been better pleased than with all the others put together."

When a message had to be delivered beyond a certain distance, the boy was given ten cents extra. This money he considered his own, to be spent as he wanted and not to be turned over to his parents. Occasionally there was a quarrel among the three boys as to whose turn it was to deliver a dime message. Andrew thought of a way to keep peace.

"Let's pool the dimes," he said. "At the end of the week we can divide the money between us, share and share alike."

Davy and Bob liked the idea so well they made Andrew their treasurer. The plan would have worked well if the candy store next door had not agreed to let them run an account. This meant a boy often owed more than his share of dimes at the end of the week.

"I won't be responsible when you spend more than your share of the money," Andrew said to Robert Pitcairn.

"Ah, Andy," the boy replied. "I have live things in my stomach that gnaw at my insides if they are not fed sweets."

The other boys thought Andrew was stingy because his

own dimes were so seldom spent at the candy store, but he knew how each penny was needed at home. Whenever something new had to be bought, some garment to replace an old one, a piece of furniture or a cooking utensil, it was such a serious matter that there was a family discussion about it, with Andrew taking part. There was also the debt to Ella Ferguson that must be paid. Every silver half-dollar that could be spared was put away in an old stocking, but it would take long to save the two hundred half-dollars they owed.

Two more messenger boys were hired at the telegraph office. Andrew, who had been there the longest, could be spared now and then to watch the downstairs office, when Colonel Glass was out. The work was easy enough. He had only to accept the messages that were brought in and send them upstairs to the operating room. Those that were telegraphed in from other parts, and copied down, he gave to the other boys to deliver. The Colonel was a popular man, with political ambitions, and when he saw that he could leave his office in capable hands, he began staying away for longer periods at a time. Andrew was spending as much time in the office as in delivering messages, but he still had the chores of delivering night messages on alternate evenings and sweeping the office floors on alternate mornings.

He became curious about the telegraph machines. Only six years before, Samuel Morse had sent the first message, "What hath God wrought!" over the wire from Baltimore to Washington. Now every city of importance had its telegraph office clicking messages from one part of the country to the other. Andrew began playing with the keys in the morning, before the operators arrived, when it was his turn to sweep. He learned how to spell out his name in the code. He pressed a key that opened an electric current miles away to guide a steel pen over a soft paper tape, writing dots and dashes, and he saw the steel pen in the Pittsburgh office move in reply. Before long he was exchanging messages with boys from other stations who were experimenting as he was.

One Saturday evening at the end of the month, the messenger boys stood in line, as usual, to receive their pay. Andrew was at his place at the head, but when he reached out his hand, Colonel Glass waved him aside and motioned for the boy next in line to step up. Andrew's heart sank when he saw David, then Robert, then the two new boys receive their money and walk out the door. What had he done? he wondered. Or was it something he had not done? Would he be told now that he was not needed any longer? How could he break the news to his parents? He was a disgrace to them as well as to himself. He saw Colonel Glass motion for him to come behind the counter, and he slowly obeyed, waiting in silence to know his fate.

"You are worth more than the other boys," the Colonel said. "I've decided to raise your pay to $13.50 a month."

Andrew's head swam. He could think of nothing to say; he simply looked on as the money was being counted out. As soon as it was in his hands he dashed out, forgetting, in his excitement, to thank the Colonel. He ran across the bridge as fast as he could. Because there were too many people in his way on the narrow footpath, he ran along the inside track, dodging buggies and wagons. What a surprise this would be for his parents! He wanted to shout the news as soon as he reached the door. But no, he would wait and tell them tomorrow. It would be a special Sunday gift for them.

He gave his mother $11.25, as he did every month, trying hard to hide his excitement. The rest he kept in his pocket. Two dollars and a quarter! It was a fortune to him. His dreams began to soar again. That carriage for his parents was coming a little closer. Some day there might even be a visit back to the old home in Scotland. Nothing was impossible now.

The next morning he put on his Sunday clothes and joined the family for breakfast. Without a word he put two silver dollars and a quarter down on the table before his parents. They looked at him in astonishment. Even when he explained about the raise, they could not quite realize it was true. Tears came to the mother's eyes.

"It's no more than you deserve," she said.

William Carnegie, a man of few words, said nothing, but Andrew could not fail to see the look of pride in his eyes.

# CHAPTER III  "A Working Boy Without a Trade"

Pittsburgh was beautiful under a newly fallen snow. The untidy rubble of its streets and vacant lots were hidden, and everything was clean and sparkling. The beauty was all too brief, like the color of a sunset or a bird's wings in flight. The coal soot from mills and factories came settling down, and with the tramping of feet, the snow turned to black slush and mud.

The slack water of the river opposite the Carnegie home sometimes became frozen over, perfect for skating. Tom and his playmate Henry Phipps joined the other children of the neighborhood, and the air was filled with merry shouts as they glided, rolled and tumbled. Andrew saw the place only when it was dark and quiet, on his way to and from work, except on Sundays. To the stern Scottish people of the neighborhood any kind of amusement on the Sabbath was frowned upon. Even reading was forbidden, with the exception of religious books. But at fourteen a boy is not ready to give up the fun of his childhood. Andrew spoke to his parents about skating early on a Sunday morning. They thought it over seriously.

"I can see no harm in it," the mother said, turning to her husband for his approval.

William Carnegie agreed. The boy had little enough time for pleasure, working as he did from dark to dark the other six days a week.

"I believe it will be all right, Andra," he said, "but I hope you'll be back in time to go to church with me."

The church of the Carnegies and the Morrisons was the Swedenborgian Society that had been formed by a group in Allegheny City. Many of the members, like Aunt Aitken, were former Presbyterians, and still clung to the strict church discipline of John Calvin. No doubt there were many who shook their heads in disapproval at the fun the Carnegie lad was having on the Sabbath, skating in winter and swimming in summer.

A walk on Sunday afternoon was something different. Even good Aunt Aitken, pious as she was, could see no harm in a quiet stroll to the edge of town. Andrew and his friends of the neighborhood went out often on a hike to a favorite grove of trees near Wood's Run, where they sat down to rest in the shade and talk, as boys will, about their dreams and ideals.

Friendship meant much to Andrew Carnegie, and the friends he made in his boyhood he was to keep for the rest of his life. On workdays there were Davy, Bob, and the new boys Oliver and Moreland. On the Sunday hikes there were John Phipps, the shoemaker's older son; and Tom Miller and William Cowley, the three who had taken the course in double-entry bookkeeping with him. Two other boys, James

Smith and James Wilson, were also in the group. Like Andrew, all had left school early to go to work, and they had the same inquiring mind and eagerness for knowledge. They formed a debating society, which was the fashion of the time. "The Original Six," they called themselves. Their meetings were held at the Phipps home after supper on a weekday evening when Andrew did not have late duties at the telegraph office. In a room that was a workshop during the day, among shoe lasts and scraps of cloth and leather, they took sides on such subjects as "Should the judiciary be elected by the people?"

They read poetry aloud, and books they owned were passed from one to another until it was returned to its owner dog-eared and worn. A book was a luxury to boys who had to contribute to the support of their family. Andrew read a paper to his friends that he had written on the subject of "Labor." Man should eat by the sweat of his brow or not at all, he said. Idleness should be dethroned and Industry crowned in her stead. It was high time the idle drones occupied the lowest position in society. A workingman was a more useful citizen, and should be respected more than an idle prince.

Here was the old cry of his childhood, "Death to privilege!" He wanted to send the article to a newspaper. Perhaps he could become a writer. He might some day even own his own newspaper.

Tom Miller told the group about a private library that had been opened to working boys. The library of four hundred books was owned by a Colonel Anderson, who lived not far from the Millers. A book could be borrowed from him on a Saturday afternoon and kept for a week, and when it was returned another could be borrowed to take its place. There was one drawback. To Colonel Anderson, the term "working boy" meant a boy who worked with his hands.

Now the young debaters had another subject under discussion. If Andrew were still a bobbin boy, and if John Phipps had taken up his father's trade as shoemaker, they would have been allowed to borrow books. To Andrew it wasn't fair that they should be left out. He composed a letter and sent it to the morning Pittsburgh *Dispatch*, urging Colonel Anderson to allow messenger boys, office boys, and clerks also to borrow his books. "Although we do not now work with our hands, some of us have done so, and we are really working boys," he wrote.

A few days later there was an answer in the newspaper columns defending the rules, saying that the term "working boy" meant one that had a trade. This was a challenge to Andrew to follow with another letter, which he signed "A Working Boy Without a Trade." The answer to this was a notice on the editorial page of the *Dispatch*. "Will the 'Working Boy Without a Trade' please call at this office."

Andrew lost no time in calling. He had won his point. Colonel Anderson's library was open to him and his friends. Books that had been beyond their reach were now theirs for the borrowing. It was as if a window had been opened in the wall of a dungeon, Andrew felt. He browsed along the shelves, reading the titles and trying to decide which one of the four hundred he wanted. A new dream began to form in his mind. "While reveling in these treasures," he wrote in his later years, "I resolved that if ever wealth came to me, I'd establish free libraries so other poor boys might have this opportunity also."

He knew the poetry of Robert Burns and he knew the works of Sir Walter Scott. Now, for the first time, he was reading essays by Charles Lamb and by his fellow Scotsman Macaulay. Wherever he went he carried a book in his pocket, snatching every spare minute to read it. He chuckled over passages from Charles Lamb:

> I have no ear. —I even think that sentimentally I am disposed to harmony. But organically I am incapable of a tune. I have been practicing "God Save the King" all my life, whistling and humming it over to myself in solitary corners; and am not arrived, they tell me, within many quavers of it.

This might have been written about himself. As well as he loved music, he could never carry a tune. He sang in the choir of the Swedenborgian Society, but he suspected the choirmaster accepted him more for his enthusiasm than for his voice.

When he finished one book, he looked forward for the rest of the week to Saturday afternoon when he could borrow another. He read Bancroft's *History of the United States,* and new heroes joined the company of Bruce and Wallace.

Until this time, all that Andrew had known about Shakespeare's works were the few selected pieces in his school reader that he had had to memorize. A celebrated actor, Edwin Adams, came to Pittsburgh to give a series of performances. He was playing Macbeth when it was Andrew's time to deliver a message to the theater. Andrew was allowed to go upstairs to the second tier to see the play. The curtains parted to show three witches on a barren Scottish heath. Scottish soldiers of ancient times, and three of Scotland's kings, Duncan, Macbeth, and Duncan's son Malcolm, came alive before his eyes. This same Malcolm was the one who had built the tower in Pittencrieff Glen, as well as the oldest part of the Abbey at Dunfermline, and he was the first of the kings to be buried there.

Andrew listened breathlessly. This was more than a story of Scotland to him. He had never until then realized what magic lay in words. Through the voice of Edwin Adams, Macbeth spoke of " 'innocent sleep, Sleep that knits up the ravell'd sleave of care . . .'

> "Tomorrow, and tomorrow, and tomorrow,
> Creeps in this petty pace from day to day
> To the last syllable of recorded time . . ."

There had been little of music in Andrew's life except in the sweet, plaintive voice of his father singing ballads of Scotland, and the short selections of oratorios in the Swedenborgian hymnbooks, though music was later to become his greatest love. In the plays of Shakespeare he found rhythm and melody in words alone, and it was like another language to him. He borrowed all the plays of Shakespeare from Colonel Anderson, and he was surprised to find how easy it was to memorize long passages.

The boys of the Original Six were invited to join the Webster Literary Society, a group of some of Pittsburgh's young intellectuals. At the same time another group of men met twice a week at the home of the young musician

Stephen Foster, in Allegheny City, to practice singing in harmony. Some of Foster's songs, such as "Old Uncle Ned," were written for this group.

The Webster Literary Society held debates, and each member in turn made a talk on a given subject. The books Andrew borrowed then were for information on the subjects discussed. The only experience he had had in public speaking was before the Original Six, his friends of the neighborhood. He gave a great deal of thought to the way he would speak before this new audience. Flowery orations with many gestures were the fashion of the time. Andrew thought of his Uncle Bailie Morrison, whose high-pitched, impassioned voice could bring hope and courage to the most downtrodden of his listeners. He had had no idle words or ornate phrases. He had spoken only from the heart, and he believed sincerely in all that he said. This became Andrew's rule too. He would talk, and never orate. He would make himself feel at home with his audience, talking *to* them and not *at* them. He would be himself, as Uncle Bailie had been, with no pretense at being someone else. He found it easy to talk with enthusiasm and hold the attention of his audience when he spoke of the things he believed in, the dignity of labor, and freedom and equality for men.

When Andrew was sixteen he had his picture taken with his brother Tom. Photography was new then, and one can imagine the mother's pride as she looked on while the boys took their pose, like a laird's sons having their portraits painted. Andrew's cravat was arranged just so, and Tom's right hand was placed carefully over the left. Tousle-headed Tom, with Andrew's arm protectively about his shoulder, looked out on the world with a shy, self-conscious smile. There was something of his father's gentle nature in his expression. Andrew's face was young for his years. His eyes, set far apart, were the eyes of a dreamer, looking far beyond the present, but the mouth and chin showed strong determination.

A copy of the photograph was sent to Scotland and passed among the relatives. The correspondence was still kept up between Andrew and Dod, with notes from Uncle Lauder from time to time. Andrew gave them news of the family and told of his own work.

Early one morning, when he was sweeping the floor of the operating room, a call came over the telegraph. It came with such persistence that he knew it must be urgent, and he ventured to answer it. It was Philadelphia calling with a death message for Pittsburgh, to be delivered immediately.

"Can you take it?" The pen moved over the running slip of paper in dots and dashes.

"I'll try, if you send it slowly," Andrew punched out his answer.

He copied the coded dots and dashes, translating them into words, and hurried out to deliver the message. It was not until he returned that he realized the seriousness of what he had done: taking it upon himself to do the work of an operator. When Mr. Brooks came into the office, Andrew told him about it. To his surprise Mr. Brooks complimented him. "But take care," he said, "if it should happen again, be sure you make no mistakes."

After this, Andrew was called upon often to watch the instrument when the operator was absent. He read the codes aloud as they came over the paper tape, and the copyist wrote them down in long slanting strokes that could be easily read. The operator was glad enough to get out of work whenever he could, with someone to take his place, but the copyist grumbled about having to do copying for a messenger boy.

It was said there was a telegraph operator in the West who had taught himself to read a message by sound alone. When Andrew heard about it, he began practicing it himself. It surprised him to learn how easy it was to translate into letters and words the long and short clicks as they came over the wire. The copyist, in a bad mood one day, threw down his paper and pencil, refusing to copy anything more as long as a messenger boy sat at the machine. Andrew shut off the running paper tape, picked up the pencil and pad the old man had thrown down, and began writing the message from the sounds of the machine. The copyist looked on in astonishment.

"Give me back my pencil and pad!" he shouted.

There were no more complaints after that.

A call came in from the office at Greensburg, a town about thirty miles away. The operator there wanted to take a leave of absence for two weeks, and asked if someone could be sent to take his place.

"Do you think you can do this work?" Mr. Brooks asked Andrew.

Never one to admit there was anything he couldn't do, Andrew replied that he felt sure he could.

"Well, we'll send you out there for a trial," Mr. Brooks said.

For the first time in his life, Andrew left his family and went off alone. At sixteen he felt himself a man of the world. He rode in the mail coach, stayed at a hotel, and had his meals in a public dining room. Knowing he was there on trial, he took his responsibilities seriously. Early every morning he was in the office, and he stayed until late at night in case some important message should come through. One stormy night, when he was alone in the office, lightning struck close to the keys and knocked him off the stool. This gave him a fear of thunderstorms that lasted all his life.

When he returned to Pittsburgh, he found himself something of a hero to the other boys. A new operator was needed, and Mr. Brooks sent a telegram to the general superintendent, James Reid, recommending Andrew Carnegie for the job. Reid had taken notice of Andrew, perhaps because he too was from Dunfermline, and he sent back the reply, "I highly approve of Andy if you consider him competent."

"I liked the boy's looks, and it was easy to see that, though he was little, he was full of spirit," he wrote later of Andrew Carnegie.

In a letter to Dod, Andrew told about his promotion. "I feel confident I will see Dunfermline again, for I can easily manage to save as much money if I behave myself well," he said.

The winter of 1852 was one of the coldest in Pittsburgh history. The unemployed stood shivering in lines for soup and bread handed out by the societies of charity. William Carnegie lost his job in the cotton mill and went back to weaving damask cloth no one wanted. Andrew's apprentice days were over, and now that he was doing a man's work, the $25 a month he earned was the main support of the family. The savings of silver half-dollars slowly grew until the time came at last when two hundred of them were counted, and the debt to Ella Ferguson Henderson was finally paid.

A letter came from Uncle Lauder about plans to build a memorial to Andrew's beloved hero, William Wallace. It would be on Stirling Heights, at the spot overlooking Bannockburn, where Wallace and his men had swept down and sent the English fleeing to the border. They would build it in the form of a tower, with winding stone steps leading to the top, and a half-way hall to be called the Hall of Heroes. If Andrew could afford a contribution, Uncle Lauder added, it would be appreciated.

This called for a family discussion. They might be able to spare a few dollars, the mother decided. Andrew was by then earning $30 a month. When the list of contributors was printed, with the name of Andrew Carnegie included, there was not a prouder woman in the world than Margaret Morrison Carnegie. As for Andrew, he knew how it felt to be a philanthropist.

He was by now taking down all the messages that came over his machine by sound alone. This was so unusual at the time that people came into the office just to watch him. Translating the long and short sounds, he relayed news from over the world to the Pittsburgh papers. Louis Napoleon was crowned Emperor of France. Turkey and Russia were close to war, with English sympathy on the Turkish side. Daniel Webster died. Henry Clay died. The Duke of Wellington died. Franklin Pierce, the Democrat, won the presidential election over the Whig candidate Winfield Scott.

Though it would be five years before he reached voting age, Andrew followed the campaign closely. He described the candidates in letters to the relatives in Scotland. "You would laugh to see how they have to bow to their sovereigns *the People,*" he wrote. He called himself a free-soil Democrat, explaining that they were for the abolishment of slavery. But both candidates, he was sorry to say, were warriors. "When I am a man I think I would like to dabble in politics."

Sometimes in a storm, when the wind shook and rattled the wires, and the rain and snow pelted down on them, the coded sounds were lost. The operators had to fill in the gaps by guesswork and intuition, work for which Andrew was especially fitted, with his keen interest in all that was going on.

The Territory of Washington was formed, separating it from Oregon. More land was acquired through a treaty with Mexico, down to the Rio Grande in southern Arizona and New Mexico, for the Southern Pacific Railroad. New Orleans had another yellow-fever epidemic. A ship bound from San Francisco went down at sea with seven hundred lives lost. A new word had been invented. *Telegram* came to be used instead of *telegraphic dispatch* or *telegraphic communication.*

Pittsburgh had its own news to send out to the world. The railroad connection between Philadelphia and Pittsburgh, once looked upon as an impossible dream, was now completed. There had to be a change of trains on each side of the Allegheny barrier, but engineers were working to solve that problem. When Andrew was in Greensburg, he had seen the deep cuts and embankments made by the Pennsylvania Railroad. Every morning on his way to work he had watched the progress as the line came closer, foot by foot. Then he saw the first locomotive brought by canal from Philadelphia and unloaded from a scow in Allegheny City. There was a big parade to celebrate, and everyone was in a holiday mood.

A new sound was heard in Pittsburgh. Through the hum and roar of mills, the clatter of horses' hoofs, the cries of street vendors, and the whistle of steamboats, there came the mournful wail of the locomotive. In the four years the Carnegies had been in America, they had seen more changes than their people had seen in a lifetime in the old country. Andrew had become so American by now that he had lost his Scottish accent. Mr. Sloane, the weaver from Dunfermline, came through Pittsburgh on his way to the West. He laughed at the way Andrew pronounced *sow crae*, the Scotch word for pigsty. Try as he would, Andrew could not say it as a true Scotsman would. "But although I cannot say *sow crae* just as broad as I once could, I can read about Wallace, Bruce and Burns with as much enthusiasm as ever," he wrote to his Uncle Lauder.

This was in the year 1852, the year of the great flood. The Ohio River, so gentle in summer, began to rise when the snow melted on the mountains. The waters grew muddy and stirred restlessly, and still the rain poured down from the darkened sky. For three weeks it rained almost without a stop. Both rivers rose high, rushing with the fury of wild beasts bent on destruction. The water came over the banks, seeping into houses in its path, covering streets and fields, blotting out the red and green colors of the earth. It came into the house where the Carnegies lived, rising as high as the downstairs ceiling. William Carnegie took his loom up to the living quarters above, and the family stepped into rafts or skiffs from the attic window to come and go.

Telegraph wires were so damaged that all communications were held up between Steubenville and Wheeling, a distance of about twenty-five miles. Andrew was sent to the Ohio town to take over all messages between the East and the West. Every hour or so he sent dispatches in small boats down the river to Wheeling, where they were wired west. The returning boats brought dispatches for him to wire east.

Late one evening he went down to the Steubenville River landing to meet the Pittsburgh-Cincinnati packet. William Carnegie was a passenger on it, taking his pack of woven table linen to sell in Cincinnati. Andrew's heart ached to see his father traveling the long distance as a deck passenger because there was not enough money to spare for cabin fare. A feeling of helplessness came over him, and he groped for words that would not come. All he could think of was that old symbol of his boyhood dreams.

"Well, Father, it won't be long before you and Mother will ride in your own carriage," he said.

The father, sensitive and shy about showing his feeling, grasped his son's hand and said simply, "Andra, I'm proud o' ye." There was an expression on his face that Andrew was to see many times in memory. Then, as if ashamed of showing his emotion, he went on, in a voice as stern as he could make it, "Now, run on back to your work and don't bother about me."

Perhaps he had some foreboding as he watched Andrew, a lad of seventeen, turn back to take on the responsibility of a man. William Carnegie had less than three years of life ahead of him.

# CHAPTER IV  First Dividends

The waters subsided, and the river, now within its banks, rushed faster than when the flood was at its crest. The earth had a sour smell in all the shady places, and over the scattered puddles left behind, clouds of blue butterflies hovered. There was a line of dead brown leaves on trees and bushes to show where the water had been. The green above the line was so lush the leaves seemed painted on. Spring vegetables that had started coming up in vacant lots and back yards were withered now and covered with mud and slime. Thick mud had to be scraped off with a hoe from the floors and walls of houses where the water had stood, and everything was scrubbed and aired.

Uncle Hogan decided to sell his property on Rebecca Street. He wanted $700 for the house and lot, but because it had been damaged by the flood and in need of repairs, he could find no buyer. He offered it to the Carnegies for $555, if they could give him $100 in cash and pay the balance in two years. Andrew and his parents talked it over,

With his brother Tom in 1851.
*(Brown Brothers)*

1861.
*(Brown Brothers)*

Steel magnate.
*(Underwood & Underwood)*

Philanthropist.
*(Brown Brothers)*

ABOVE, The coaching party, 1880. Andrew Carnegie holds the reins; his mother is seated beside him. *(Brown Brothers)* BELOW LEFT, Andrew Carnegie (left), with his cousin George Lauder and his friend Thomas Miller. Taken in Glasglow, 1862. *(Brown Brothers)* BELOW RIGHT, Henry Phipps (left), Andrew Carnegie, and John Vandervort, during their 1865 walking tour in England. *(Culver Pictures, Inc.)*

Margaret Carnegie.
*(Brown Brothers)*

Mrs. Andrew Carnegie.
*(Brown Brothers)*

Mr. and Mrs. Andrew Carnegie.
*(Culver Pictures, Inc.)*

The Carnegie cottage in Dunfermline. *(Carnegie Corporation)*

Skibo castle. *(Carnegie Corporation)*

weighing one decision against the other. It would not be easy. The interest alone, which must be paid twice a year, would be hard enough to raise, and there would still be the principal to pay. Prices in this country were high for food and clothes, twice as high as in Scotland, but rents were also high.

"So very high," Margaret Carnegie said.

She pointed out that tradesmen had to pay $6 to $8 a month for a four-room house like the Hogans', with nothing to show for it at the end. The family decided to take the risk, and buy. They moved to the larger house and turned the small one in the back of the lot over to Aunt Aitken, rent free, as she had done for them when it was hers.

Margaret Carnegie bought a new bureau and a rocking chair that Christmas, for the little furniture they had was not enough for a house of four rooms. She kept on with her work of binding shoes, cloth top boots laced up the back or front or side, fur-lined winter shoes, soft, fragile slippers of satin or velvet for dainty ladies who seldom walked. And on Saturday nights she helped Aunt Aitken, who with another Scotswoman had opened a grocery store.

"I'm sure we can have the place paid for in two years," she said. "And when that's done, we'll be in easy circumstances."

Andrew wrote about all this in a letter to his Uncle Lauder. He rather guessed, he said, that when the house was paid for, his mother would be needing new carpets or something else.

"Father is in good health, and he has about $70 worth of cloth which he intends to sell as soon as the good weather sets in," he went on. "He is highly delighted with the Caloric

Ship just now, and looks forward to the time when steam will be among the things that were."

He told of the test run the ship had made from Norfolk by sea to New York on power supplied by hot air. "It will soon visit your shores, another monument of American genius."

The mother interrupted from time to time with something else she had thought of to tell the relatives in Scotland.

"Mother thinks that I have never told you that we had bought Uncle Hogan's house and lot, but I'm pretty sure I did," he added in a postscript.

The most important news in the letter was that he had left his job at the telegraph company on the first of February, in 1853, and was working for the Pennsylvania Railroad, which had opened a Pittsburgh office with the coming of the first train.

"I have met very few men that I like so well in this country, and I am sure we will agree very well," he said of his employer, the jovial young superintendent, Thomas Scott.

The acquaintance began before the Railroad Company's own telegraph line, running alongside the track, had been finished. Thomas Scott had often gone to the telegraph office where Andrew was working, to be in direct communication with his superior, Mr. Lambaert, the general superintendent at Altoona. There was something about the boy's personality, and the efficient way he went about his work of sending and receiving messages, that impressed him.

"Mr. Scott asked me if I thought you'd care to come and work for him," Scott's assistant said to Andrew one day. "I told him that wasn't possible. You wouldn't want to quit your job as operator to become a clerk."

"Not so fast," Andrew had answered. "You go tell him he can have me."

He had been thinking for some time that if a better offer came to him, he'd take it. He liked the work at the telegraph office well enough, but the time had come when he must give some thought to his future. The highest he could go in this kind of work would be as manager of some office, with a salary of perhaps $700 or $800 a year. Was this as high as his dreams could soar? No, his place was at the top, and he must get there.

The change had been made after another family council. Even the father had made no objection. Colonel Glass, who had replaced Mr. Brooks as manager of the telegraph office, had been the one to advise Andrew against taking the new job. When he learned that Mr. Scott had offered a salary of $35 a month, he said he would pay $400 a year, but Andrew had made up his mind. The salary wasn't so important as the opportunity the new job offered. He would have made the change even for less money.

Andrew liked the hours of his work at the railroad office. Instead of having to stay until ten or eleven every other night, he was through for the day at six o'clock. The trains ran on a single track, and the superintendent had to know each time the different trains passed a station. Outside of that, there was little to do at the telegraph instrument. The rest of Andrew's time was spent at clerical work, such as writing letters and auditing accounts.

Mr. Scott had an office fixed up for his own use and took Andrew in with him. Until it was finished, they worked in a room shared by the railroad laborers. Railroading was new at that time, and many of the workers were from the crews

of riverboats. They brought the coarseness of the riverfront
with them, swearing, drinking, scuffling. Like the other men
connected with the railroad, Andrew copied their way of
dress. He thought it was manly to wear high boots of cowhide, and a shirt opened at the collar, with no necktie. He
laughed with the other men when someone came into the
office wearing kid gloves. Even at eighteen, however, he felt
uncomfortable over the coarse language of the workers, and
the way they chewed tobacco and spat out the juice. He was
*scunned,* he said, using a Scotch word for disgust, and he
made a vow he'd never swear and never use tobacco in any
form. How different these men were from John Phipps,
Tom Miller, or any of the other boys of the Original Six!
Men such as these railroad workers were the ones Margaret
Carnegie had in mind when she drove Uncle Hogan's
brother out of her house for suggesting Andrew sell knickknacks along the waterfront. But they were not bad at heart,
Andrew felt. He discovered a kindness beneath their swag-
gering and their rough, boisterous talk, a kindness in many
cases that he was never to forget.

One of the duties in his new job was to go to Altoona for
the monthly payroll and checks. His first trip started out
well. He was fascinated by the train, and was allowed to
ride in the cab with the engineer.

At Altoona, Andrew saw a city in its beginning. The Railroad Company had bought land here four years before.
There were a few company-owned houses and shops, with
others under construction. The Greek Revival house of
Baker, the ironmaster, stood on a hill overlooking the new
town.

Robert Pitcairn had also left the telegraph office to work

for the Pennsylvania Railroad. He was in Altoona, a clerk
for Mr. Lambaert, the general superintendent, and he introduced Andrew to his employer. Andrew was awed and ill-
at-ease before this stern, aloof man. After a few words of
greeting, Mr. Lambaert surprised him by saying, "You must
come down and take tea with us tonight."

He could only stammer some kind of acceptance, and he
both dreaded and looked forward to visiting in the home of
such a prominent person. Mr. Lambaert put him at his ease
at once by introducing him to his wife with the remark,
"This is Mr. Scott's Andy." Nothing could have pleased the
boy more, for Mr. Scott was a hero to him. Mrs. Lambaert,
sensing Andrew's shyness, was tactful and tried to make him
feel at home.

The next morning he started back to Pittsburgh with the
payroll package under his arm. Again he rode in the cab of
the engine. Looking through the treetops down in the valley
below, he could see lonesome little cabins perched, like doll
houses, on the hillslope. Children stood in the doorway waving a hand or shyly staring, while dogs barked furiously and
horses reared high in fright. The rails were of wood, faced
with strap iron, and fastened to granite blocks. The train
jerked and jolted like a bucking bronco over the tracks, and
the engine puffed and blew out sparks from the wood fire.
Suddenly Andrew had an uneasy feeling. He reached for the
payroll, and it was gone.

"I've lost it!" he shouted to the engineer. It must have
been shaken from him within the last few miles. "Can you
back up the engine so I can look for it?"

In spite of schedules to be met, the good-natured engineer
backed the train while Andrew's eyes searched anxiously

along the tracks. At last he saw the package lying on the banks of a large stream, only a few feet from the water. He ran down and grabbed it and looked inside. Everything was there, just as he had received it. But what a narrow escape! Suppose it had fallen a few feet beyond! It would have been swept downstream and he would never have found it. Suppose, also, the engineer had refused to back the train! It would have changed his whole life. Mr. Scott would never have trusted him again, nor would anyone else who heard about his carelessness. Luck was with him that time. "But don't do it again," he said to himself. Only the engineer and the fireman knew what had happened, and they kept his secret. After that, the payroll package was held so tightly in his hands, when he returned from Altoona, that nothing could have shaken it loose.

That was not the last risk he took that might have changed his entire future. Early one morning he arrived at the office to learn over the wires that there had been a serious accident on the Eastern division, which held up a passenger express train heading west. There was always danger of confusion and wrecks on a single-track line when one train broke down or jumped the rails. The eastbound train was moving slowly and cautiously, with a flagman walking ahead to signal at every curve. The freight trains in both directions were all standing still on the siding. The workmen on these trains had waited all night, and Andrew knew they were tired and eager to start moving. No one but the superintendent could give a train order, but Mr. Scott was not to be found. Andrew was tempted. He had wired Scott's orders often enough to know what should be done. However, if he took it upon himself to give orders in the superintendent's place, and it resulted in a wreck, he'd not only find himself in disgrace; he'd have to stand criminal punishment.

"But I can do it. I know I can," he said to himself.

He waited a little longer for Mr. Scott; then, finding himself still alone, he sat at the keys and began giving orders in Scott's name. The trainmen, little suspecting they were following the instructions of a clerk, started the trains moving. Andrew listened intently to every click of the telegraph to know the position of each train, and he gave orders that carried them along from station to station. At last everything was running smoothly again, and he gave a sigh of relief. Tom Scott, who had just heard about the delay on the track, came rushing into the office.

"Well, how are matters?" he asked. As, without waiting for a reply, he took up a pencil to write his orders, Andrew realized the seriousness of what he had done.

"Mr. Scott," he said hesitatingly, "I couldn't find you anywhere, so I gave these orders this morning in your name."

"Are they going all right? Where's the Eastern express?"

Andrew showed him the messages and gave him the position of every train on the line, the eastbound train, the passenger express, and the various freight trains. Tom Scott looked over the answers of the conductors and the latest reports from the stations where a train had passed. Andrew could feel the older man's eyes upon him, but he dared not look up. There was silence. Again Scott went over all the reports, examining them carefully; then, without a word, he returned to his own desk. The next morning, and for many mornings thereafter, he was at the office before Andrew arrived. Later, Andrew learned from the freight agent how Mr. Scott had felt about what he had done.

"Do you know what that little towheaded devil of mine did?" he had said to the freight agent the evening after the event. "I'm blamed if he didn't run every train on the division without the slightest authority."

"Did he do all right?" the agent asked.

"Oh, yes, all right."

He began to give Andrew more responsibility, letting him give most of the train orders, though Scott's initials, T.A.S., were still used. The president of the Pennsylvania Railroad heard about the train-running incident. Before this, when he had come on his inspection trips from Philadelphia he had walked through the office, taking no more notice of Andrew than if he had been part of the furniture. Now he paused at the telegraph instrument where Andrew sat.

"So this is Scott's Andy," he said with a smile.

Andrew's salary was increased to $40. Every month when he brought back the payroll from Altoona, he found in it two $20 gold pieces for himself.

The Horseshoe Bend over the mountain barrier was completed, and the trains came in straight from Philadelphia, without making a change. The first one, called the Lightning Express, made the run in thirteen hours. That was twenty-seven miles an hour. Only a horse could go as fast! A bridge was being built across the Mississippi between Rock Island, Illinois, and Davenport, Iowa, and railway lines were extending farther and farther west. Men had visions of some day connecting the Atlantic and the Pacific coasts.

Almost three years had passed since Andrew began working for the Pennsylvania Railroad. In October, the month before his twentieth birthday, his father died, leaving him head of the household.

"He was kindness itself, one of the most lovable of men," Andrew said of him later. "Not much of a man for this world, but a man all over for heaven."

There were medical and doctor bills for the father's last illness, in addition to meeting the payments on their home. David McCandless, a member of the small Swedenborgian Society, sent for Aunt Aitken and asked if her sister needed financial help. He scarcely knew the Carnegies, but he offered to advance whatever amount she thought necessary. Margaret Carnegie was too proud to accept, but Andrew was never to forget the man's generosity. With the money he earned and his mother's wages for binding shoes, they managed to get along, and keep Tom steadily in school.

One morning a man came into the railroad office when Andrew was in charge, alone, and asked for work. He was a blacksmith, with a family to support, he said, and was out of a job. Thoughts of his father must have come to Andrew, and he could not turn away a man who was asking only leave to toil, to provide for his family.

"We haven't anything in Pittsburgh to offer you," he said, "but there may be a job in Altoona. Wait, I'll send a telegram and find out."

The answer came back that there was an opening for a blacksmith in their shops. Sensing that the man had no money for the fare, Andrew gave him a railroad pass to take him there.

Thomas Scott saw the struggles Andrew and his mother were having, and he thought of a way to help.

"Do you have $500 to put in a good investment, Andy?" he asked.

Five hundred dollars! Andrew Carnegie had scarcely five hundred cents he could call his own, but if Thomas Scott recommended an investment, he knew it was a sound one. The station agent had ten shares of Adams Express stock he would sell, Scott went on.

"I think I can manage that sum," Andrew said.

There must be a way, he thought. That night he talked it over with his mother. Nothing was impossible to Margaret Carnegie. When it had seemed they could not come to America because of the $100 more they needed for passage, she had found a way, by borrowing it from a friend.

"Five hundred dollars," she mused. They had paid that much into their home. The father's sickness and death had delayed them, but now there was only a little more to pay, and they would be out of debt. "We might borrow the money and pledge this property as security."

The next morning, dressed in her widow's black, she took the steamer for East Liverpool, where William Morris, her brother, was justice of the peace. When she returned the next day, she had $500 in her purse, and a mortgage on her home. Andrew turned the money over to Mr. Scott, only to learn there was another problem facing him. He would have to put up another $100 as premium.

"You can wait and pay that when it is convenient," Mr. Scott said.

On a Sunday afternoon not long afterward, Andrew and

his friends went for a hike to their favorite place, the grove near Wood's Run. One was missing from the Original Six. John Phipps had been killed by a fall from a horse, and since then the group had drawn closer together. Andrew took from his pocket a white envelope addressed to Andrew Carnegie, Esquire, with the round stamp of the Adams Express Company in one corner. The boys laughed with him over the word *Esquire* after his name. From the envelope Andrew took out a check for $10, his first month's dividend from the stock he had bought. The check was passed around among the amazed boys. Ten dollars a month from an investment of $500! None of them, including Andrew, had ever earned a dollar except through hard work. This seemed unbelievable, and they wanted to know more. They made a pact that they would save as much as could be spared from their salaries, and watch for another opportunity such as this, in which they would all share.

There were serious discussions on those Sunday afternoons in the grove. They talked about the mysteries of life and death, the here and the hereafter, and they had long theological talks about men's ideas of God. They were reading Darwin and Herbert Spencer, and they rebelled against the relentless, vengeful God of their ancestors. Each stage of civilization creates its own idea of God, they said, and the God they worshiped was kind and forgiving, as a father is to his children.

"All is well, since all grows better," Andrew Carnegie said, and he declared this would be his motto from then on.

He was sure there would come a time when men would no longer kill their fellow men on the battlefield. ". . . one of the most important points to be gained is to render war and its instruments abhorrent to the young," he wrote in an article for a Sunday-school paper when he was eighteen:

> If each was educated to look upon these machines made expressly for the destruction of his fellow-men with the same horror that they behold the scaffold and the guillotine, if these could be seen only in museums as relics of a barbarous age instead of their likeness being paraded in religious newspapers, how long would such scenes as that enacted at the Heights of Alma take place to shake our belief in Man's possessing anything in common with his God. Let war be shown to the young men in its true light and all will be well.

Andrew's friends were as interested in politics as he was. Election year was drawing near, and the question on everybody's tongue was whether slavery should be allowed or forbidden in the new states and territories. There were outbreaks of violence. A slavery party sacked the town of Lawrence, Kansas, and John Brown led his antislavery men against the Missourians at Osawatomie.

When Andrew was seventeen, Uncle Lauder had suggested that Andrew and Dod carry on a debate through letters about the merits of the American and British systems of government. Andrew had been delighted.

"It will, no doubt, be beneficial to both of us to examine into the systems of Government by which we are ruled, and it will prompt us to read and reflect on what, perhaps, we would never have done without that stimulant," he wrote. "I have therefore accepted Dod's challenge, and am now reading the Early History of our Republic, and I find that the obstacles which our revolutionary fathers had to surmount and the dangers they had to encounter were far greater than I had imagined and are worthy to take place among the deeds of Scotland's heroes."

Dod called the United States the most tyrannical country in the civilized world. Andrew knew he had in mind the slave question, but he could not let this remark go unchallenged.

"I know that the laws and institutions of this country will compare favorably with any other nation on earth, at least as far as I have seen, and except the relation of Master and Slave, they are a century in advance of European."

A new political party, called the Republicans, was formed by the defeated Whigs and dissatisfied Democrats. In 1856 they held a preliminary convention in Pittsburgh, at Lafayette Hall. Andrew stood with the crowds on the side of the street watching the notables, in broadcloth frock coats and high silk hats, ride by in open carriages. John C. Frémont, the explorer of the Far West, was nominated as their candidate for President. The name of Abraham Lincoln, a rising young lawyer from Illinois, was mentioned for Vice-President, but failed to win.

With the Scot's burning love for freedom, Andrew followed the campaign speeches of the new party. He wrote again to his Uncle Lauder about his interest in politics.

"I have the characteristics of 'our folks' rather strongly developed (as Aunt Aitken would say) and of course therefore, am a great—or rather small—dabbler in politics."

He was a firm abolitionist. Not only should slavery be abolished; something should also be done about the loose system of states' rights. However he felt about independence for Scotland, he wanted for his adopted country one solid,

all-powerful central government. There should be uniform
laws for all states, laws of railroad supervision, control of
corporations, marriage, divorce. He composed a letter expressing these views, and sent it to Horace Greeley, editor
of the New York *Weekly Tribune*. Seeing his words in print
brought back the old ambition to become a writer on political affairs.

Frémont was defeated by James Buchanan, a Democrat.
This did not still the political unrest in the country. There
was a sense of foreboding, of something about to happen
that could not be prevented. Men argued about free or slave
territories and tariff laws. Friends of a lifetime became bitter
enemies.

Letters written by Andrew Carnegie began to appear
often in the newspapers, not only on politics, but on other
subjects as well. He wrote about the city's attitude toward
the Pennsylvania Railroad, and this was given a prominent
place in the Pittsburgh *Journal*. The morning it appeared,
a telegram came over the wires for Thomas Scott, from
Mr. Stokes of Greensburg, the chief council for the Railroad. Andrew copied the message as it came in. "Find out
from the *Journal* editor who wrote that article in this morning's paper."

The editor could not know who wrote it, for the article
was unsigned, but he could show the letter to Mr. Scott, and
Andrew knew that his handwriting would give him away.
He might as well admit the truth, he decided, and when he
gave Scott the message he confessed that he was the author.
Thomas Scott looked at him in astonishment and some
doubt. The pen was a mighty weapon indeed, Andrew
thought.

"I read the article this morning and wondered myself who had written it," Scott said.

The letter led to a friendship between Mr. Stokes and Andrew Carnegie. The first time Andrew was invited to visit the older man, he was ushered into a library more magnificent than any he had ever visualized. He had lost some of the shyness he felt on that first visit with Mr. Lambaert in Altoona, but he stood speechless before the great marble mantel, with an open book carved in the center of the arch. He read silently the words carved on it:

> He that cannot reason is a fool,
> He that will not is a bigot,
> He that dare not is a slave.

He vowed again that he'd have a library of his own some day, and over the mantel those words would be carved.

Thomas Scott was promoted to take Lambaert's place as general superintendent at Altoona, and he took his valued clerk with him. The move was no doubt a welcome one for Scott, for his wife had died a short while before. He left his children with relatives in Pittsburgh until a suitable house could be found for them. Andrew was also searching for a house so that he could send for his mother and Tom to join him. In the meantime, Andrew and his employer took a room in a hotel.

The trainmen were in a rebellious mood when they arrived, and there were mumbled threats of a strike. Andrew was awakened one night and told that the freight-train men had left their trains at Mifflin. The line was blocked and all traffic stopped. Thomas Scott, tired and anxious, had fallen into such a deep sleep that Andrew hardly had the heart to waken him. He half opened his eyes at the sound of Andrew's voice, scarcely hearing what he was saying.

"Would you like me to go up there and see about it?" Andrew asked.

Scott murmured his consent, and Andrew left at once for the office. There he talked to the men gathered before him, reasoning with them in Scott's name. They were persuaded to go back to their trains when he promised them a hearing the next day, and traffic on the lines was started again.

The shopmen became restless. They were secretly organizing, and tension was felt wherever they gathered. Andrew felt that the problems facing Scott as he was taking up his new duties were caused by jealousy at his promotion. Late one night when Andrew was walking back to the hotel from the office, he heard footsteps behind him. He realized that he was being followed, and turned around to see who it was. A man, lurking in the shadows, moved up closer.

"I mustn't be seen with you," the man said in a low voice, "but you did me a favor once, and I was determined if I ever had a chance to repay you, I would."

In the darkness Andrew could see the dim outline of a familiar face. He recognized him as the blacksmith he had helped to find a job.

"I've got a good job, and my wife and children are here with me. I've never been so well off in my life," the man went on. "Now I want to tell you something for your own good."

The shopmen were signing their names to a paper, he said, threatening to strike on the coming Monday. With this information Thomas Scott was able to act. Notices were posted in the shops that the men who signed the paper were to be dismissed, and they could call at the office for their pay. The strike was broken and the trains were kept running.

Railway trains were fast replacing canals for traveling east and west. One lawsuit followed another, in disputes over land grants and right of way. Cattle, once so terrified of the first locomotives, strayed unconcerned along the unfenced right of way and along the tracks. Many an angry owner went to court and sued for damages because a hog or cow had been run over. Lawyers on both sides won reputations arguing cases in these disputes. Abraham Lincoln won a famous decision for the Illinois Central. Stephen A. Douglas was a lawyer for the same company. The brilliant Mr. Stokes was kept busy defending the Pennsylvania Railroad against suits.

A lawsuit came up, to be tried in Greensburg, and there was talk of Andrew being called up to testify as principal witness against the company. Stokes asked for a postponement, and advised Scott to send Andrew out of the state as soon as possible so that he would not be summoned. Andrew was delighted with this unexpected vacation. With a pass that would take him anywhere on the line, he decided to visit his friends Thomas Miller and James Wilson, of the Original Six. They were in railway service also, and were stationed at Crestline, Ohio. He boarded the train and took a seat at the end of the last car. A man dressed in homespun clothes came and sat down beside him. He had the red face of a farmer, and in his hand he carried a small green bag.

"My name is Woodruff," he said. "The brakeman told me you were connected with the Pennsylvania Railroad."

After Andrew Carnegie introduced himself, the man opened his green bag and took out a model of a section of what he called a sleeping car, something he had invented.

"It is for night traveling," he said.

The importance of this flashed through Andrew's mind at once. Railroad lines were expanding so that there would come a time, he knew, when travelers could go long distances that would take several days. Sleeping cars with berths would add so much to their comfort, he could foresee a great demand.

"I'll have to wait until I return to Altoona to speak to the general superintendent about it," he said. "Can you come there if I send for you?" Woodruff said that he would.

Andrew could scarcely enjoy his stay in Crestline, so impatient was he to tell Scott about Woodruff's invention. He could not get out of his mind the thought of having sleeping cars on the Pennsylvania line. Scott was interested, as Andrew had felt sure he would be, though he called it taking time by the forelock. He sent for Woodruff, and a contract was drawn up between the two men. The company would place two of the inventor's sleeping cars on their line as soon as they could be built.

"Would you like to join me in this venture?" Woodruff asked Andrew after the contract was signed. "If so, I'll let you have an eighth interest."

The offer came as a surprise to Andrew, but he accepted without hesitation. The cost would be paid in monthly installments after the cars were delivered. Andrew had such faith in the invention that he was certain he would need only to pay for the first installment. After that, the sleeping cars would pay for themselves. His eighth share of that first payment was $275.50. The only way he could raise that amount was to go boldly to the local banker and ask for a loan. Mr. Lloyd, the banker, was a tall man, towering over Andrew by about a foot. He put his hand on Andrew's shoulder.

"Why, of course I'll lend it. You're all right, Andy."

The sleeping cars were the success Andrew knew they would be, and his share of the monthly earnings was enough to meet the payments as they came due. He made another investment at that time, $400 worth of stock in the Monongahela Insurance Company, which also paid for itself in dividends.

Andrew bought his first horse, which he named Dash. This was another step toward that cherished dream of a carriage. Mrs. Carnegie and Tom were now with him. Andrew had found a large house for them, in a pleasant part of the Altoona suburbs. They still kept the house on Rebecca Street. Uncle Hogan had died, and Aunt Hogan with her daughter Maria came back to live in the house she had once owned as Aunt Aitken had done.

Thomas Scott was with his children in a house next to his office, with a door connecting the two buildings. His niece, Rebecca Steward, had come from Pittsburgh to keep house for him. The neighbors, seeing Mr. Carnegie and Miss Steward riding by, were sure there'd be a marriage before long. Andrew, too, dreamed of a wife with the charm and poise of this young woman. She was his idea of a perfect lady, acting as hostess for her uncle when he entertained guests.

His mother should have had this kind of life, he thought, with leisure for reading and visiting and entertaining. She had given up binding shoes before she left Allegheny City. The foot-treadle sewing machine, invented by Mr. Singer a few years earlier, had been improved upon. One had been made for shoemakers that could sew through leather. This did not mean that Margaret Carnegie was idle. She was always the first one up and the last to go to bed, and her hands were never still the whole day. With a long checked apron tied around her waist, she fanned the banked ashes of the hearth and stove, built up the morning fire, and then made the porridge and mixed batter for the bread. On her knees with pail and scrubbing brush, she cleaned the floors. She boiled clothes in an iron pot over a back-yard fire, rubbing them on a board; she drew water for the rinsing, and then hung them out to dry. A fire had to be built in the stove for ironing. Holding the handle with a padded cloth, she wet her finger to test the heat of the iron. After a few minutes of ironing, it was cool and had to be changed for another on the stove. She had supper ready for her sons when they returned home, and at the end of the day she sat mending and sewing until it was time to bank the fires for the night and go to bed.

Andrew was earning $65 a month, and his investments were beginning to bring in a nice sum to add to it. They could afford to have a more social life, and their home should be a place where they could entertain friends. First they must hire a servant, someone young and strong who could take over the heavy work of the house. But he reckoned without his headstrong mother. A stranger coming into her house and taking over! She wouldn't hear of it. This was her life. Who else could iron the ruffles of her sons' linen shirts or cook scones and pancakes the way they liked! Over her protests a girl was hired, but she left soon afterward.

Another came to take her place; then she too left, no doubt in tears.

Andrew saw that tact was needed. "Mother," he pleaded, putting his arm around her, "you've done everything for, and you've been everything to, Tom and me. Now let me do something for you."

It would be as if they were partners, always thinking what was best for each other, he said. After all, he and Tom were no longer children, needing her full attention.

"The time has come for you to play the lady," he went on. "Some of these days you are to ride in your carriage. In the meantime do get someone in to help you. Tom and I want you to."

Reluctantly, his mother agreed to let someone come into the household to help with the work. Perhaps she realized, for the first time, that her son was getting on in the world. To please him she began going out to visit with the neighbors, and to have them in for a cup of tea. The carriage Andrew had talked about from the time he was a little boy bringing in water from the public well no longer seemed so impossible. It is certain, however, that Margaret Carnegie kept a critical eye on the way her sons' shirts were ironed and the kitchen floor was scrubbed.

# CHAPTER V  District Superintendent Carnegie

In 1859, three years after the move to Altoona, Thomas Scott was appointed vice-president of the Pennsylvania Railroad. After his return from the interview in Philadelphia, he called young Carnegie into the private room of his house, which opened into his office. Everything was settled, he said. He would soon be moving his family to Philadelphia, and Enoch Lewis, the division superintendent, had been named his successor. Andrew waited with mingled emotions to hear what else he had to say. Would he be allowed to go as Mr. Scott's assistant, or would he be left behind? They had been associated together for seven years, and a close friendship had developed between the two in spite of the difference in their ages. To stay on, working here under someone else, seemed unbearable to Andrew.

"Now about yourself, Andy." There was a pause, and to Andrew every heartbeat was an eternity. "Do you think you could manage the Pittsburgh division?"

"I think I can," the answer came promptly.

Did he *think* he could manage it! He *knew* he could.

There were times when he felt that nothing was impossible for him to do, but he was surprised to know that others had faith in him. The present superintendent at Pittsburgh had been promoted to the transportation department in Philadelphia, Mr. Scott went on.

"I recommended you to the president, and he has agreed to give you a trial. Now, about your salary. What do you think that should be?"

Andrew Carnegie, who from childhood had known the anxiety over having enough money for the family needs, had not thought about salary in connection with this new job. At twenty-three, he would have a department of his own to manage, the same position Thomas Scott had when he first came to work for him. The orders he'd give would be signed with his own initials, A.C. instead of T.A.S., as they had been.

"Salary!" he exclaimed. "I'm not thinking of salary. It's the position I want. You can make it whatever you like. I'll be satisfied with the same salary I'm getting now."

"When I had that position I was getting $1,500 a year," Scott said.

Andrew well remembered, for it had seemed a fortune to him when, at seventeen, he brought back the monthly payroll from Altoona. He had wondered what Mr. Scott did with all that money.

"The superintendent there now has been getting $1,800," Scott was saying. "Suppose, then, we start you at $1,500 and raise it to $1,800 later on, if you make good."

The winter was severe the year Carnegie took up his duties as district superintendent. For days at a time the skies were dark with snow clouds, and icicles fringed the eaves of shops and houses. Accidents and wrecks followed one after the other that winter. The lines had not been built for the heavy traffic now rolling in, and the equipment, though less than ten years old, was already outdated and inefficient. The cast-iron chains holding the rails in place snapped and broke like twigs in the ice storms, sometimes as many as forty or fifty a night. Andrew drove the men under him mercilessly, and he drove himself still harder.

Tom, who had studied telegraphy in Altoona, was with him in the office, sitting at the desk that had once been his, and working as his clerk. Carnegie Brothers! It wasn't quite the same as he had once dreamed, but it was a start. Tom was capable and reliable, though he was not one to take the risks that Andrew had taken. He would never take it upon himself to give orders, in Andrew's name, to start trains rolling after a wreck.

The Carnegies had not gone back to their home on Rebecca Street, where the two aunts were then living. They rented a house across the river on Hancock Street, closer to Andrew's office.

Margaret Carnegie, even with all her energy, must often have wondered at the endurance of her older son. He worked day and night that winter. Once, for a week and a day, he had not even time to take off his clothes, and slept only in half-hour snatches in some boxcar. Tom remained at the keyboard in the office, ready for any message that might come in telling of another broken line. The mother could only see that fresh clothes were ready, the water hot for a bath, and warm food waiting when they did return.

Gradually the ice melted and the hardened earth began to thaw. The snow clouds disappeared, but the Pittsburgh sky was no brighter. In the past three years more trains than ever were passing through the city, puffing smoke and cinders. More coalpits and ironworks were sending up showers of sparks around the city's edge, with a thick smoke that came rolling in like a dark curtain that covered the earth and shut out the sun. It settled on streets and houses and into the lungs of all who breathed it. Soot irritated the skin and gathered in the hair. A hand that touched the balustrade of a stair became black, and faces that were scrubbed with soap and water were as grimy as ever within an hour. Washing on the line was ready for the tub again before it was dry.

Mr. Stewart, the freight agent, told Andrew about a house that was available; it adjoined his own property at Homewood Estates, in the hills outside Pittsburgh, where homes, set in plots of five to twenty acres, were built by those who could afford to escape the city's smoke.

With this move a new life opened for the Carnegies. Margaret Carnegie, who had missed the clear air of Altoona, again had a garden of her favorite flowers, and there was the comforting sound of chickens in the barnyard. From the windows she could look out on wooded valleys and quiet country lanes. There were birdsongs again, and the sound of running brooks, and shade trees with the play of light and shadow through their foliage.

Andrew and Tom made new friends among their neighbors. Stewart, the freight agent, took Andrew to call at the mansion of Judge Wilkins, who had once owned all the land of Homewood, and gave the place its name. Andrew, as a messenger boy, had delivered messages to him. Now he knew him as a friend, and became acquainted with his wife and two daughters. They were courteous and hospitable, with a way of making him feel drawn into the family circle.

There were musical evenings, or charades and theatricals, with the young people of the neighborhood taking part. At other times there were quiet evenings of conversation and discussion.

These evenings at the Wilkinses' played an important part in the mind of a self-educated young man. When a subject unfamiliar to Andrew Carnegie came up for discussion, he made it a point the next day to find out all he could about it. He was constantly learning something new, with one thing leading to another. He listened to music, played on the pianoforte or violin, of the modern young German composers, Schumann and Brahms, and he read with the group poems by Robert Browning, just then becoming known, and Alfred Lord Tennyson. A charade of Niobe weeping for her children, or Shelley's poem "Prometheus Unbound," was enough to start him reading the myths of ancient Greece. This led to Greek philosophy, and on to the story of Rome. When someone quoted a line from Emerson's essay "Self-Reliance," he wanted to read the whole essay.

"Is it so bad then to be misunderstood? Pythagoras was misunderstood, and Socrates, and Jesus, and Luther, and Copernicus, and Galileo, and Newton, and every pure and wise spirit that ever took flesh. To be great is to be misunderstood." If some among these great names mentioned by Emerson were unfamiliar to Andrew, he lost no time in reading everything he could find about them. He began at this time to reach for goals of a higher value than the carriage of his early dreams.

Before the move to Homewood, young Carnegie had met and called upon Miss Lelia Addison, whose mother had come from Edinburgh. "A wee drap o' Scotch bluid atween us," they said of themselves, but there the kinship ended. These people belonged to another world. They had never known the pinching poverty, the struggle for even the plainest food, the mended clothes washed at night to be ready to wear the following day. Thomas Carlyle had been Mrs. Addison's tutor when she was a girl in Scotland, and she had sent her own daughters to be educated abroad. They impressed their young admirer by speaking Italian, Spanish, and French as fluently as they spoke English.

Lelia Addison, daintily dressed in the latest fashion, with flounces and bows and flowers on her wide hoopskirt, frowned on the rough clothes Mr. Carnegie wore. For her sake he gave up the heavy cowhide boots and wore low shoes of soft leather laced up the sides. He had a frock coat made of English broadcloth, and a vest of silk brocade. With these he wore a high hat and even the kid gloves which he once thought foppish. They went for rides in a buggy rented from a livery stable, Miss Addison holding a ruffled parasol against the sun. When her companion made a mistake in grammar, she promptly corrected him, and if she thought his voice too loud, she urged him to speak softly, as a gentleman should. Andrew began watching his manners, and through her influence he became gentle and courteous.

Tom Miller, still with the railway service, was transferred from Crestwood, and he moved to Homewood, in a house close to the Carnegies. Rebecca Steward's brother was also a close neighbor. Friends were necessary to Andrew Carnegie's existence, and once he made a friend, he never lost him through any fault of his own. He had not seen Dod for twelve years, yet they kept up a regular correspondence.

The miles that separated him from Thomas Scott made no difference in their friendship. Andy, Davy, and Bob, the messenger boys, were still close friends. Bob was with the Pennsylvania Railroad, and Andrew was soon to put Davy in charge of his telegraph department. Once more the three would be together in their work. The Original Six still kept in touch with one another. Now new friends were added to the old: the Wilkins family; Mr. Coleman, the ironmaster, and his family; the Vandervort brothers, John and Benjamin. When there were musical evenings John played the violin and Andrew sat listening with half-closed eyes, lost in the enjoyment of it. Sometimes, on a summer night, the young people sat outdoors, singing the popular songs of the day to the accompaniment of John's violin. If Andrew sang off key, the sound was lost in the chorus of voices, the call of the whippoorwill, the hoot of owls, and the croak of frogs from the near-by pond.

The year 1860 was an exciting one. The Prince of Wales visited the United States and Canada. It was the first time in history a direct heir to the throne of Britain came to the New World. The Emperor of Japan sent ambassadors to this country, after three hundred years of isolation from the rest of the world. The first run of the Pony Express was made between Sacramento, California, and St. Joseph, Missouri. The horses were changed every ten miles, at 190 relay stations. The oil well drilled the year before at Titusville, near Pittsburgh, was bringing in a thousand barrels a day, in a never-ending stream. Boom towns were springing up, and prospectors were drilling small wells everywhere in the Pennsylvania fields.

More exciting than any of these events to young Carnegie

was the presidential election. The Republican party had a meeting in Chicago to choose their candidate. On the third ballot the nomination went to the tall, gaunt lawyer from Illinois.

Stephen Douglas, the fiery little candidate opposing Lincoln, split the Democratic party when he came out against secession. The southern Democrats put up another candidate, and still another ran for a party called the Constitutional Union. Feelings ran high. Southern states were threatening to secede. That meant either war or a divided nation. The Wilkinses and others among the new friends at Homewood were closely connected with southern families, and their sympathies were for the South. Andrew Carnegie was too ardent an abolitionist to keep quiet about his beliefs. The old cry "Death to privilege!" had now become "Free Soil! Free Homesteads! Free Territory!" He came into the Wilkinses' drawing room one day to find the family excited about a letter just received from the grandson, Dallas, who was attending West Point.

"What do you think!" the gentle Mrs. Wilkins said to Andrew, "Dallas writes that he has been compelled by the commandant to sit next to a Negro. Did you ever hear of the like of that! Isn't it disgraceful? Negroes admitted to West Point!"

"Oh, Mrs. Wilkins, there's something worse than that," Andrew said with a mischievous smile. "I understand that some of them have been admitted to heaven."

A dead silence followed this remark. At last Mrs. Wilkins spoke gravely, "That is a different matter, Mr. Carnegie."

Newsboys called out the headlines the night after the election. Pennsylvania, with 70,000 votes, went for Abraham

Lincoln. New York gave him 50,000 votes. The news came over the wires from one state and then another. Abraham Lincoln had won the election. Guns boomed, cannon roared, and men marched in torchlight parades, waving banners proclaiming the new President-elect.

In the following month South Carolina carried out her threat, and seceded. Mississippi followed two weeks later.

"If the great American people only keep their temper on both sides of the line, the trouble will come to an end," Lincoln said when he stopped at Pittsburgh on the long journey by train from Springfield to the White House. "And the question which now distracts the country will be settled, just as surely as all other difficulties of a like character which have originated in this government have been adjusted."

By this time five more southern states had seceded from the Union. "Let the erring sisters depart," Horace Greeley wrote. "All hail Disunion! No Union with slaveholders," said another. The President-elect was urged to deal with a firm, unyielding hand. The quiet voice of Abraham Lincoln spoke on the day of his inauguration:

"Physically speaking, we cannot separate. We cannot remove our respective sections from each other, nor build an impassable wall between them."

There would be no interference with slavery where it existed, he said. But the Union must be preserved whatever the cost.

In the South, the Confederates began seizing United States forts and arsenals. There was a demand for the surrender of Fort Sumter in South Carolina, six weeks after the inauguration. This was refused, and the first shot of the Civil War was fired in the bombardment of the fort. President Lincoln called for 75,000 militia from states by quotas. This brought about the secession of Virginia, Arkansas, North Carolina, and Tennessee. For a month the country waited in an agony of suspense, fearful of what would happen next.

One Sunday Carnegie sat in the library of Mr. Stokes, the counsel for the Pennsylvania Railroad. As he and the older man were discussing politics, he faced the mantel with the inscription that had once so impressed him: "He that cannot reason is a fool, he that will not is a bigot, he that dare not is a slave."

"I cannot agree that the North has a right to use force for the preservation of the Union," Mr. Stokes said.

Quickly Andrew jumped to his feet. "Mr. Stokes," he said, "we'll be hanging men like you in less than six weeks."

This outburst was greeted with good-natured laughter.

"Nancy, Nancy, listen to this young Scotch devil," he called to his wife in the adjoining room. "He says they will be hanging men like me in less than six weeks."

Six weeks from that time Mr. Stokes, through the influence of young Carnegie, was to become a major in the Federal Army, and lead his volunteer troops into battle to preserve the Union.

# CHAPTER VI The Railroads of War

In the spring of 1861, at the outbreak of the war, Andrew Carnegie was called to Washington. Secretary of War Cameron, the Pennsylvanian, had appointed Thomas Scott Assistant Secretary of War, with the title of Colonel. Since this was one of the most important departments, in the beginning of the war, Scott chose Carnegie as his assistant in charge of the military railroads and telegraphs of the government.

A Massachusetts regiment, the first to answer Lincoln's call for volunteers, had been attacked a short while before, by an angry mob of southern sympathizers, as they passed through Baltimore. The insurrectionists then seized the telegraph office, and for several days the nation's Capital was cut off from all communication with New York by rail, mail, or telegram.

Carnegie's first duty was to see that troops could get through safely to Washington by another route. Under Scott's orders, he organized a force of railway men, and took the train at Philadelphia for Annapolis. From there a branch line ran to the junction, where it connected with the main line. Carnegie and his men were kept busy for several days repairing this branch line and making it passable for heavy trains. They succeeded in having it ready by the time the tempestuous General Butler arrived at Annapolis with several regiments of troops, impatient to push on to the Capital.

The first train started forward cautiously, with Carnegie in the cab of the engine, his eyes on the track ahead to watch out for any sign of a break. They reached the main line safely, but when they were a short distance from Washington, Andrew saw a place where the telegraph wires had been pinned to the ground by wooden stakes. He had the engine stopped, and got out to release them. He hadn't noticed until too late that the wires were pulled to one side when they were staked. They sprang forward as they were released, striking him full in the face. He was knocked down by the blow, with a bleeding gash in his cheek. It was in this condition that he reached Washington, among the first, he said, to shed his blood for his country.

Colonel Scott gave him his next orders. There had to be a way of getting the troops across the river into Virginia. For a week Carnegie worked night and day with his men. They extended the tracks of the Baltimore and Ohio Railroad from its old depot along Maryland Avenue, to the Potomac. Long Bridge had to be rebuilt, and a ferry was put in service, so the trains bearing soldiers could cross to the other side.

Andrew Carnegie was stationed at Alexandria, seeing that the lines were extended still farther into Virginia. He worked outside during the heat of midsummer, when the sun shone mercilessly from a cloudless sky. Wild roses that were blooming in the fields and the flowers of the jimson weed folded their petals at midday, and the songs of birds came faintly from the distant forest, scarcely heard above the hum and drone of summer insects. One day a feeling of dizziness came over Andrew. His heart pounded and his head ached, and he thought he would die of thirst. He felt burning hot and at the same time he shivered with cold. Some of the workers who had known southern summers realized that he had sunstroke. They took him to a shady spot under a tree, loosened his clothing, and gave him water from their canteens, a swallow at a time. When the fever had passed, Carnegie went on with his work, thinking little about it. There was a satisfaction in knowing that he was serving the country that had done so much for him.

The armies on both sides were biding their time, each waiting for the other to attack, as neither wanted to be the aggressor. In both the North and the South there were some who still hoped the differences could be solved peacefully, without bloodshed. Others were impatient for action. Eighty days had passed since Fort Sumter was fired on and had to be evacuated. "On to Richmond!" came the cry in the North. Lincoln hesitated and was criticized. He knew the problem the North still faced in transporting men and supplies to the battlefields.

"On to Richmond!" the soldiers under General McDowell took up the cry when they crossed the river into Virginia on the Saturday of July 20th. Carnegie saw them as they passed through Alexandria, raw young recruits from farms or shops or factories, with no experience in soldiering. They had enlisted for a period of three months, time enough, they thought, to whip the Rebels and put them in their place. A group of spectators followed them, wanting to see the victory from a distance. There were senators and congressmen among them, riding in carriages as if on a pleasure jaunt.

The next day, Sunday, Andrew was in the telegraph office of his headquarters. Reports were coming in, which his operators relayed to Washington. The troops had crossed Bull Run near Manassas, to find the Confederates, under Beauregard and Johnston, waiting for the attack. Beauregard was being pushed back. They were driving the enemy back toward Manassas. The morning reports were encouraging. Then, in the late afternoon a message came that was unbelievable. McDowell and his men were in full retreat. The day was lost. Now it was a matter of saving Washington with what was left of an undisciplined army.

"We must rush every engine and car to the front and bring the men back," Carnegie said to his men.

The trains could get only as far as Burke's Station. There Carnegie helped load train after train with wounded volunteers, mud-caked and soaking wet from a steady downpour of rain. More than ever he was struck by the brutality of war. The mock battles he and Dod had fought with paper helmets and wooden laths, took no account of suffering and dying. Even in the letters and articles he had written against war, he had thought of it abstractly. But here were men who, two days before, were healthy and strong and in high spirits, and now they were brought back bleeding, moaning, and crying out in pain. Almost three thousand had been killed or wounded, youths who had had dreams and plans for the future, as he had. The same was true on the other side of the battlefield. Surely, he thought, there was a better way for nations and factions to settle their differences.

"Suppose you go to war, you cannot fight always," Lincoln had said in his inaugural address. "And when after so much loss on both sides and no gain on either, you cease fighting, the identical old questions are again upon you."

The sound of the Confederate guns came closer. Carnegie and his operators returned to their headquarters in Alexandria on the last train, to find the town in a panic. The spectators had come rushing back first, with mud-spattered faces and wild, frightened eyes. Soldiers who had escaped the enemy guns came next. They had been up since two in the morning, and had gone into battle before they had a chance to eat. They came running from all directions, staggering from weariness like drunken men. Many had thrown away their guns when they found them in the way.

All during the night the guns of the Rebel forces could be heard. Andrew Carnegie went into the messhall the next morning and looked about with some misgivings. Would he find his men there, he wondered, or had they too deserted, as so many were doing? A few conductors and engineers had managed to get boats and had crossed the Potomac, but he was pleased to see how many had remained at their posts compared to other branches of the service. And of the operators, not a one was missing.

Orders came for them to return to Washington. There they found as much confusion as at Alexandria. A gloom had settled over the whole city. The Confederates were expected to attack at any time, and they could have succeeded then if they had tried. Some demanded peace, and others called for more action. The volunteers, seeing that the war would not be over as soon as they expected, were deserting by the hundreds. At the White House, an anxious President sat up all night, making plans to reorganize his forces.

When Carnegie saw the condition of the nation's Capital, his heart sank. There was old General Winfield Scott, the commander in chief, so feeble it took two men to help him from his office to his carriage. He had fought well in the Mexican War fourteen years before, and better still in the War of 1812, but now, at seventy-five, he sat dozing in his office all day. General Taylor, his commissary chief, was little better.

Thomas Scott and Andrew, as his assistant, had to deal with such men as these in the matter of supplying transportation and transporting troops. They had to wait days before any decision could be made on matters that needed to be acted upon immediately. Carnegie, then twenty-five, looked around, amazed that there was scarcely a young, active officer at the head of any department. How could the Union survive with such men in charge? he wondered. General McClellan had been summoned to Washington the day after Bull Run and put in command of the army, but as long as old Winfield Scott was in the way there was little he could do.

Andrew Carnegie could see no conflict in his hatred of war and his wish to see this war fought to the finish. Once begun, there was nothing to do but go on to victory or give up in defeat.

The railway and telegraph departments of the government were an important part in the war effort. They were able to run efficiently when Secretary of War Cameron authorized Scott to do what he thought was necessary with-

out waiting for the slow decisions of the officials. One of
the busiest rooms in the War Building was the telegraph
office. The Secretary of War came to wait for replies to his
messages. The Secretary of State came also. Sometimes a
tall, familiar figure, the President himself, walked into the
room and sat at the desk, anxious for the latest information.

The first time Andrew saw Lincoln, sitting in silence, his
face in repose, he thought he was the homeliest man he had
ever laid eyes upon. No wonder all his portraits were so like
him. With those deep seams and ridges, and features so
marked they seemed carved out of granite, an artist would
find it impossible not to paint a likeness. His complexion
was swarthy, and his hair and beard were coarse black.
There was something, however, that the portraits did not
show. This was the sparkle of his face when he spoke. His
gray eyes shone with a light that reflected a spirit so beautiful that one forgot the features. There was no aristocratic
pomp about him. He had a kind word for everyone, even
the youngest boy in the office, and he was as courteous to
a messenger boy as to a Secretary of State. Never had Andrew seen a great man who so thoroughly made himself one
with all mankind. He was completely the democrat, he
thought, showing in every act and word the equality of men.

Discouraging reports kept coming in after the summer
had passed. The Federals raided a Confederate camp at
Ball's Bluff across the Potomac in October, and were badly
defeated, with almost three times as many casualties on the
northern side as on the southern. In November General
Grant routed the Confederates in Belmont, Missouri, but
reinforcements from Kentucky compelled him to withdraw.

Since the night of Bull Run, Abraham Lincoln had been

working out a military policy. Evidently there had to be some changes made. In December old General Winfield Scott was persuaded to resign and let the younger McClellan take command. The three-month soldiers who refused to serve longer were discharged, and new volunteers were called for. For the Cabinet posts, there should be trained men instead of the politicians the President had been persuaded by his advisers to appoint. Secretary Cameron was the first to go. Soon after the New Year he was sent as Ambassador to Russia. Another Pennsylvanian, Edwin M. Stanton, was chosen as his successor.

Thomas Scott and Carnegie continued their work under the new Secretary. Carnegie admired the man, and a friendship was formed at this time that was to last through the years. But, true to his nature, his loyalty to Cameron remained the same. There was talk of graft and incompetency in the War Department under him. Congress debated whether or not to approve his appointment as Ambassador to Russia because of the way he had mismanaged affairs in Washington.

"If other departments had been as well managed as the War Department was under Cameron, all things considered, much disaster would have been avoided," Carnegie was to say later.

In a war that was fast spreading, Scott and Carnegie had been able to organize the entire system of military transportation, and the telegraph system was operating efficiently. Like the three-month soldiers, they had only temporary appointments. It had been thought that the war would be over in three months, and now a year had passed. Thomas Scott was needed at his old post in Philadelphia.

When he left, Carnegie returned to Pittsburgh to take up his duties as district superintendent.

The war had made Pittsburgh an important railroad center. Troops moved through from the Northwest and West by hundreds of thousands. Freight loads of munitions added to the strain on the Pennsylvania line. Andrew Carnegie had never fully regained his strength after the sunstroke of the past summer, and now he began to feel the effects of overwork. He had never before known what it was not to be healthy and full of energy. He became seriously ill for the first time in all his twenty-six years. Even after his recovery he could scarcely drag himself through the day's work. The time came when he had to give up and ask for a leave of absence. He thought of Scotland with the cool mists and the wind blowing in from the sea. Fourteen years before, when he left there, the dream of returning seemed as hopeless as a voyage to the moon. Year after year, when it was time for the bluebells to bloom or for the broom to color the fields, he had felt an ache in his heart. Now the dream was no longer impossible. He would go back to Dunfermline.

Ten minutes after receiving word that a leave of absence for six months had been granted, he was writing to Dod. "We will make a bee line for Dunfermline. I won't turn my head to look at anything until I see Bruce's Monument. I remember that was the last thing I saw of Dunfermline and I cried bitterly, when it could be seen no more."

# CHAPTER VII  Bridges, Rails, and Sleeping Cars

The steamship *Etna* pulled out of New York Harbor on the 28th of June, 1862. Andrew Carnegie, his mother, and his friend Tom Miller stood on deck with their fellow passengers, watching the land slowly recede from view.

Margaret Carnegie was beginning to grow stout in these early days of her prosperity. There was a dress of black silk in her trunk. It was trimmed with pleated ruffles, with a collar of white ruffled lace. She had a gold watch and chain that she wore pinned to her bodice. This homecoming was something of a triumph to her. It had been her own decision to leave Scotland and make this move, with barely enough money to get the family of four to America, and she had gone into debt for that.

Andrew's salary of $200 a month was only a small part of his income now. His investment in the Woodruff sleeping cars alone was bringing in yearly dividends of over $5,000, and there had been other investments from time to time. Even the Adams stock, which Margaret Carnegie had mortgaged her home for, was bringing more than $100 a month.

The mother sat on a deck chair while Andrew and Tom Miller walked the deck, mingled with the other passengers, or stood together at the rail, looking out on the vast circle of horizon. Miller was now purchasing agent for the Fort Wayne and Pittsburgh line. The two friends were as full of plans and dreams for the future as they had been when they were boys. Miller had bought a third interest in a small iron mill with a master mechanic named Kloman. Recently he had divided this share with Henry Phipps, the younger brother of his boyhood friend, John, lending him the $800 necessary for the sixth interest. Kloman was a genius in forging things of iron. The axles he made for railway cars were the best, holding up under the kind of strain that would break an ordinary axle. But he had no sense of business. Phipps, on the other hand, was bright and capable, and could make a success of anything he undertook.

When the ship landed at Liverpool, Miller parted company with the Carnegies, and went his way. Andrew, true to his promise to Dod, took the first train out for Dunfermline. He and his mother sat silently looking out the window as pastures, farms, and villages rolled past. To Andrew it did not seem real, going back to the old home of his memories. It was as if this were another of the many dreams he had had of returning. As for Margaret Carnegie, whatever sense of pride and triumph she had felt was forgotten when they crossed the border into Scotland. There was only the joy of the exile returning home.

"Oh, there's the broom! The broom!" she exclaimed.

She could hold back her tears no longer. How many times she must have secretly longed for one more glimpse of the golden flowers that grew in Scotland as they grew nowhere else in the world! Andrew felt just then that he could have knelt down and kissed the very earth itself. His father should have been here, to share in this homecoming, he thought.

The relatives were waiting for them with a warm welcome. There was also that certain shyness that comes to those who meet after a long absence, a groping for further words to say, furtive glances to see what changes the years had made. Their Andy had been an adolescent boy when he left. Now he was twenty-six, a prosperous railroad executive.

"Oh, someday you'll be coming back here to live, and keep a shop on High Street," Aunt Charlotte said. This was to her as high a goal as one could want in life.

Uncle Bailie, older and grayer now, sat on the sofa beside Andrew. He started to speak; then his voice choked and his dark eyes filled with tears. He rushed from the room, and waited until he was calmer before returning.

"There's something about you that brings to mind my father," he said. "What it is, I do not know, some tone of voice, some little gesture, but it's there."

It had been arranged for Andrew to stay with Uncle Lauder and Dod while the mother visited among the other relatives. Dod, a year younger than Andrew, was now a civil engineer. They walked up the hill to the grocery shop on High Street, and Andrew's eyes took in all the familiar scenes. It was as he had pictured it so often in his mind, the hilly streets where each house looked down on the roof and chimney pots of the next one, the houses themselves, old, gray, and sturdy, the shops with outside stairs leading to the living quarters above. Even the old well still stood at the head of Moody Street. But there was a difference. Everything had shrunk to the size of a child's toys. He could almost touch the eaves of the house where he was born. And the hills surrounding the town, so steep and high and far away when he was a child, were no more than little mounds. The schoolhouse, the mansions that had once seemed so imposing, all were like doll houses. Even High Street, with its shops that, in his memory, had been as fine as any on Broadway, was like a Lilliputian street. They reached Uncle Lauder's house, and Andrew was once again in the old room where he and Dod had been taught so much. All in his nature that was poetic, romantic, and patriotic had its start here. He still felt like one in a dream.

"You are all here. Everything is just as when I left," he exclaimed. "But you are all playing with toys."

There were some things, however, that had not changed. Uncle Lauder was still a giant among men. Nothing could ever change him. The Abbey, too, remained the same. It was as magnificent as he had remembered it. When he looked up at the carved block letters on the tower's balustrade, KING ROBERT THE BRUCE, his heart was filled as when he was a child. The sound of the bells at the curfew hour was as sweet to his ears as when it had sent him racing to bed. And there was Pittencrieff Glen, the forbidden paradise it had always been, where he could still catch stolen glimpses through the open gates.

Andrew wanted to see all the friends and playmates of his childhood. There were the boys who had gathered clover for his rabbits, and there was the blacksmith's daughter whose schoolbooks he had carried when he was a boy. Good Mr. Martin, the teacher, was dead now, but Mrs. Hender-

son, the Ailie Fargie whose generosity and faith in the Carnegies made it possible for them to go to America, was still
living. She and her husband did eventually buy the home
they had been saving for. Every Christmas for the past several years, Andrew Carnegie had been sending her $100,
the full amount of the loan, calling it the interest on her
investment.

"Now I think it's about time to pay the debt in full," he
said to her teasingly.

"Don't worry about the loan, Andra," the old woman
replied with a twinkle in her own eye. "I'm well satisfied
with the interest."

"But I'm able now to pay off the principal in full."

"Dinna ye worry about the principal," she said. "It's very
well invested as it is."

Another of the old acquaintances he saw was the sailor
who, fourteen years ago, had taken Andrew away from his
Uncle Lauder and lifted him, still crying, to the steamer
deck.

"I've seen many a parting in my time," the old sailor said.
"But that was the saddest one of all."

The relatives could not have enough of asking questions.
At each gathering they must hear more about Uncle Morris, Aunt Hogan and Aunt Aitken, and about all that had
happened in the past years. Again they talked of the old
days when Andrew was a child, repeating the clever things
he used to say and do.

Uncle Lauder wanted to know more about the war in
America. He stood almost alone in this town of southern
sympathizers. Andrew told about his work in Washington
and the important part the railways and telegraph were

playing in the war. Uncle Lauder had some money saved and he gave it to Andrew to invest for him in Federal bonds. "Invest it as you think best," he said. But he added that if it were put in United States bonds, he would feel that in her hour of danger he had been of some small help to the Republic.

The crisp, pure air of Scotland and the sight of his old home and friends did not bring about the recovery for which Carnegie had hoped. A slight cold was enough to send him to bed with a high fever that lasted for six weeks. The old-fashioned doctor tried bleeding him as a cure, which made him weaker still. There were times when he hovered between life and death. Gradually, under the tender care of Uncle Lauder, the fever left him, but for a long time he was too weak to stand on his feet.

As soon as young Carnegie was well enough to travel, he and his mother left for America. This time the parting was not a sad one. They were going home instead of into the unknown, and they knew that they would come back to Scotland again. Divided as he was in his loyalties between the old home and the new, Carnegie felt the same excitement in returning to America as in going back to Scotland. On the train to Pittsburgh he looked out the window eagerly as they passed familiar landmarks. The workmen of the eastern end of his division were waiting for his train, and as it passed them, they fired a cannon as a salute to welcome him home.

Carnegie hoped to take up his duties again with the energy he had once had, but the effects of his illness lingered on. In February, five months after his return, he wrote to

Dod that he could not pronounce himself well yet: "This confounded attack will not leave me it seems. I have been exceedingly careful since I resumed duties, but I can't gain strength. Everything else is all right. The physicians all say my lungs are again restored—all that troubles me is weakness."

The winter that year was a hard one. It rained and froze and rained again. Every morning the temperature was below zero, warming up a little at noon, only to fall again in the evening. Andrew Carnegie must often have been reminded of that first winter when he was made district superintendent. Then he could work day and night without tiring. It was long before his strength fully returned. The following June he wrote to Dod that he had not yet got back to old times, but tired very easily. He bought a new horse, the prettiest in Pittsburgh, he said, and one that could easily compare in style with any in England. Tom Carnegie had his horse and buggy to ride to work, but Andrew enjoyed riding horseback the ten miles from Homewood to the office. It was excellent medicine for him, he said.

The fighting spread. Men were killing men in Tennessee and Arkansas, in Mississippi and Louisiana, in Virginia and the border states of Missouri and Maryland. There was victory sometimes on one side and again on the other, with neither side showing signs of weakening.

"Of course I am as certain as ever that the Government is to emerge triumphant and slavery to go down," Andrew said in his June letter to Dod. "I look back to Britain's history, know that America is of the same blood, and await the result with the greatest equanimity. If this is not the fight of Freedom, that principle never before required defiance and Bannockburn was a farce, for the question is essentially one of national existence. Wait a little longer!"

In spite of his slow recovery Carnegie was never so busy as he was at this time, seeing that the lines of the division were repaired and kept in good condition so there would be no lag in the movement of troops and supplies. Bridges that were burned by the enemy had to be replaced as quickly as possible. One that was burned was such an important bridge that the trains had to be held back for eight days, an appalling delay in wartime. Carnegie remembered the little iron bridge he had seen built at Altoona, and he thought of how well such a bridge could withstand fire and flood, not only during the war but in peacetime as well. He called on H. J. Linville, the talented engineer who had designed the Altoona bridge, and then he called on the mechanic who had built it, John Piper, a hustling, active man who knew his work well, and his steady thoroughgoing partner, Schiffler. He persuaded them to join him in forming a company for building iron bridges. His own work would be bringing in the orders. There was one other partner Carnegie wanted, and that was Thomas Scott. They started with a small amount of capital, and each partner paid $1,250 for a fifth interest. Again Carnegie borrowed from a bank the amount for his share.

They went by the name of Piper and Schiffler, but this was changed later to the Keystone Bridge Company, after the Keystone State of Pennsylvania. A few wooden shops were built, and they were ready for business. Carnegie felt that in Linville they had the best designer obtainable, and Piper and Schiffler were the best possible mechanics for the work.

Now they must use only the best of materials. When he heard that the Panhandle Railway Company needed a bridge across the Ohio at Steubenville, he called on the president, Thomas Jewett. Jewett was hard to convince. A bridge spanning three hundred feet over the channel, with its top cords and support made of cast iron! Could that be done? The contract was signed, but Jewett still had his doubts. He came to the shop and when he saw the piles of heavy cast iron lying about, he shook his head in disbelief.

"I don't think those heavy castings can be made to stand up and hold themselves, much less carry a train across the river," he said.

Andrew Carnegie was not worried. He had confidence in the men working on it. The designer and the mechanics would be the strictest inspectors of their own work, and if they could not build a safe bridge, they'd build none at all.

The condition of the railway lines was another matter that had been on his mind. The old rails were becoming dangerous. Repairmen were kept busy working on them, but they could not hold up much longer. Strong iron rails would be the solution. He formed another company, this one called the Superior Rail Mill and Blast Furnaces. Again he chose as partners the men best fitted for this kind of work.

Tom Carnegie by this time was one of the partners in the Kloman Iron Mills, having bought his shares with money lent him by Andrew. Large orders were coming in from the War Department for axles and gun carriages, and the firm grew prosperous. Kloman, the mechanic, resented his partners, Tom Miller and Miller's friends, Phipps and the younger Carnegie. It was his skill in designing and forging, he felt, that had built an important industry from a small blacksmith shop. First he wanted Phipps out of the firm, but Miller would not hear of it. Then he turned against Tom Miller.

Miller came into Carnegie's office one day, his eyes flashing with anger. Kloman was trying to force him out of the company. To make matters worse, Henry Phipps, whom he had befriended, had taken sides with Kloman. Andrew sympathized with his friend, and did what he could to calm him. He went to Kloman and tried to reason with him, but when this did not succeed, he suggested to Miller that they form their own company.

He matched the amount of money Miller received for his interest in the Kloman Mills. They named their new company the Cyclops Mills, and started production on a tract of seven acres. It was much more land than they'd ever need, they thought, but part of it could always be rented.

Gradually the interests of Andrew Carnegie widened. He was manufacturing iron, and making iron bridges and iron rails. With his friend William Coleman from Homewood, he visited the oil fields south of Titusville, at the place where Oil Creek flows into the Allegheny. They had gone there before, soon after Carnegie returned from Scotland, when prospectors were just beginning to drill for oil. Then it had been like some vast picnic, with everybody in high spirits. If a man could not find a place to stay, it didn't take him long to put up some kind of shanty, and away he went to his claim, and started to drill. Banners with mottoes floated from the tops of derricks. Two men were working their treadles, boring for oil on the riverbank, and on their banner they had printed "Hell or China." In everyone's mind there was the thought of a fortune within easy reach, only a hand's grasp away.

On this trip, two years later, Carnegie and his friend returned to find an orderly place, well on its way to becoming a settled town. They were serenaded by a brass band that the musical prospectors had formed.

New uses had been found for oil, which was once used only as medicine, costing a dollar for a small bottle, and hawked by medicine men. Later it was also used to grease machinery. The evil-smelling oil that had caused such misery to Andrew when he worked in the bobbin factory now was being distilled and refined, with enough of the odor removed so that it could be used instead of whale oil for lamps. Whaling ships were on their way out, and oil towns were springing up.

Carnegie and Coleman, as partners, invested in the most promising of the wells, those on the Storey farm. The price, $40,000, seemed high to them, for no one believed the supply of oil would last long. Coleman had a scheme, though, to turn their investment into a million dollars, he said. They would excavate a deep hole, large enough to hold a hundred thousand barrels of oil. When all the wells in the region stopped producing, the price would go up. At $10 a barrel, they would have a million dollars' worth of oil in storage, ready to sell.

The oil gushed forth, filling the lake to the top. Still it kept flowing, thousands of barrels a day, until there seemed no end. The two partners gave up the idea of keeping the oil any longer, and began shipping it down the river to Pittsburgh.

This investment led to another, a large well in Ohio that produced oil especially good for lubrication. Coleman and Carnegie took in a third partner.

That year Carnegie's income from the oil investments was almost $18,000. The price of stock jumped from $10 to $100 a share.

Abraham Lincoln was elected for a second term. The tide of the war had turned in favor of the North, with General Grant in command of the Union Army. The South could not hold out much longer under the long blockade, with its people starving and its soldiers undersupplied, ragged and weary.

Toward the end of that month, March, 1865, Andrew Carnegie gave up his work with the Pennsylvania Railroad. Twelve years had passed since he started as an office boy under Thomas Scott. He lay awake one night, going over in his mind all that had happened since then. One small step had led to another. He was like a mountain climber who made his goal the top of the peak, only to find a higher one in the distance, beckoning him on. He was offered a promotion as assistant superintendent, with headquarters at Altoona. If he accepted he could go on to more important positions with the railroad, as Scott had done, but he wanted to be on his own. He needed time to attend to his own growing interests, bringing in contracts for iron bridges, for rails, for oil and iron.

The war drew to its end. General Lee surrendered to General Grant on the seventh of April. With tears in his eyes he bade his men return to their homes and prove themselves as worthy in peace as they had been in war. There was rejoicing in the North, with the sound of drums and trumpets, the ringing of bells, and the joyous shouts of the people.

The next week the bells were tolling, the drums muffled, and the flags hung at half-mast. A whole nation mourned the assassination of their President.

"With malice toward none; with charity for all." The words of Abraham Lincoln were to be remembered by the defeated South, sharing the nation's grief.

Four years of bitter fighting, man against his countryman, with a loss on both sides of 600,000 men, had not stopped the expansion of the young and vigorous nation. The movement to the West went on during the war, as before. Farmers, miners, prospectors, cattlemen, and cowboys rode off to settle the prairies, deserts, and mountains that lay between the Mississippi Valley and the Pacific. Irish immigrants and discharged soldiers were laying rails and building roadbeds to take the trains farther toward the Rocky Mountains, and Chinese coolies were brought to California, where they were trained to use the pick and shovel to build a railroad to the East.

Though he was no longer with the railroad company, Andrew Carnegie's interests and energy were concentrated almost entirely on railroads. As the railroads expanded and prospered, so did he. More railroad bridges were built by his company, more rails were made, and more iron produced to go into them. The sleeping cars, in which he owned an eighth interest, could not be turned out fast enough to meet the demand. The first rails were laid for a roadbed to cross the continent, and Carnegie saw the need for more locomotives. He persuaded Tom Miller to join him in organizing a company for manufacturing them. Again he insisted on making nothing but the best.

While the Carnegie and Miller Cyclops Mill was producing iron to meet the peacetime needs, the Kloman Phipps Mills, which had expanded to supply the demands for war material, found it hard now to keep going. Tom Carnegie and Henry Phipps wanted the two firms to merge, to become partners rather than competitors. Kloman was against this move. Miller had wanted to bring Andrew Carnegie into the firm before Phipps joined it, but Kloman had objected then and he objected now. He was afraid of Carnegie, impetuous, daring, too ready to carry out new ideas and changes. Now he said that, with the share Tom Carnegie owned, the two brothers would have a controlling interest. Phipps calmed his fears. Mr. Carnegie, he was sure, would do nothing without the consent of all partners.

Andrew was in favor of merging and forming one large company out of the two smaller ones. Kloman was a great mechanic, painstaking and thorough, the kind of workman he liked to be associated with. The problem now was persuading Tom Miller. He pointed out to Miller that by combining the two firms, Miller would become the largest single stockholder. "You'll be returning a conqueror, Tom," he said. "Can't you let bygones be bygones?"

Miller could forgive Kloman, but he could never forgive Phipps, whom he had befriended and helped get his start in the business.

"I'll do anything you like, Andy, except for one thing," he said. "I'll have no personal association with my former protégé."

Carnegie, who was never one to hold a grudge, could not believe that Miller would keep resentment in his heart too long. They named the new firm the Union Iron Mills. Piper and Schiffler were also brought in as partners.

It was not long before Carnegie began making changes, as Kloman had predicted. He discovered that nothing was known about the financial position of the mills until the end of the year when stock was taken and the books balanced. This was true of all the leading iron mills of the city. No one knew the cost of various processes. Owners who would not have trusted a clerk in an office with five dollars without having a check on him, were supplying tons of raw material every day in the mills without thinking of weighing what each returned in the finished form. They were like moles burrowing in the dark, he said, not knowing whether they were operating at a profit or a loss, until the year was over.

He introduced a system of weighing and accounting throughout the works, so there would be a record of the cost of each process. They began to know not only what each department was doing, but what the men were doing as well. They discovered who was saving material, who was wasting it, and who produced the best results.

After the short depression that followed the change from war to peace, there was a prosperity in the North such as the country had never known before. The four large enterprises Andrew Carnegie started, the Keystone Bridge Company, the Superior Rail Mills, the Pittsburgh Locomotive Works, and the Union Iron Mills, were steadily growing, and everything was running smoothly under capable management. But business affairs were never to become the whole of Carnegie's life. Often he turned for companionship to the one among his friends who had the least interest in the world of business, John Vandervort of Homewood, or Vandy, as he was called. Vandy led a carefree life, taking more pleasure in playing his violin, reading, hiking with the group, than in shops or mills or factories. One Sunday he and Andrew were stretched out on the grass with a book they had taken along to read together, Bayard's *Views Afoot*. It brought back memories to Andrew of Britain's quiet country roads and villages, and he wanted to see them again. His return to Dunfermline four years before, so long dreamed of, had proved to be a disappointment because of his illness. Now his strength had fully returned, with the energy that could keep him going night and day. It was time for another trip, and this one would be a real holiday. He'd go as carefree as Vandy himself.

"Vandy," he said, "if you could make $3,000, would you spend it on a tour of Europe with me?"

"Would I!" Vandy exclaimed. "Would a duck swim! Would an Irishman eat potatoes!"

Shares in oil wells were still going up, like rockets, Carnegie said. Vandervort gave him his savings of a few hundred dollars, which Andrew invested, and before long this amount grew to the $3,000 needed for the trip. Henry Phipps was persuaded to join them.

After landing in England, the three friends, with knapsacks on their backs, set off on a walking tour. Dod came down to join them for a part of the way, and an English relative of Henry Phipps, John Franks, also became one of the group. They had no certain destination in mind. When they came to a fork in the road, they knew that whichever way they chose, it would lead to some village where they could find an inn where they could have a cup of tea, a meal, or a bed for the night. Vandy wore his letter of credit in a money belt around his waist. He was chosen treasurer for the group, and each night he counted carefully what they had spent and how much they had left.

"For we are boys, merry, merry, boys, merry, merry boys together," they sang as they tramped along the quiet roads that led from farms to villages. Red-cheeked children stared and smiled shyly as they passed. When they came to an industrial town, Andrew and Henry dropped their role of merry, merry boys and visited the iron mills, comparing the British method with their own. They looked for new improvements they could apply when they returned home. When the mail caught up with them, they opened their letters eagerly, to know how matters were at home. Their talk turned to rolling mills, furnaces, and profits.

"Great Caesar, boys!" Vandy exclaimed one day when they had stopped at a tavern. "If I ever get $1,500 a year! Great Caesar, boys!" He banged his fist so hard on the table the mugs clattered. "Fifteen hundred dollars a year! Catch me working like a slave the way you and Harry do."

Carnegie shared interests with both Vandy and Henry. He went with Vandy to art museums and concerts. At the Crystal Palace in London they heard the works of Handel performed. When the chorus sang "Hallelujah," Carnegie rose instinctively with the rest of the audience, moved by the power and majesty of the music.

When the walking tour was over, they left England for a trip through Europe. Dod stayed behind, but young Franks remained with them. They visited the great cathedrals, and were stirred by the music of their choirs. They stood before the works of the world's masters in art museums. Carnegie found himself judging paintings and sculpture by a new standard. The kind of art that was the fashion of the time, which he had once looked upon as beautiful, he knew now to be false and pretentious, compared to the truly great art.

During the trip Franks wrote in his diary, "Andy is so overflowing that it is extremely difficult to keep him within reasonable bounds, to restrain him within limits of ordinary behavior—he is so continually mischievous and so exuberantly joyous.

In Venice they visited the Doge's Palace. They saw the Senate chamber, with the throne of the Doge and the chairs once occupied by the senators. To Andrew this meant Shakespeare's *Othello,* and the scene where the Moor defended himself for having married the fair Desdemona.

There was mail for them at Rome. One letter brought news that Congress had passed an Act to encourage the building of railway lines to span the continent. The first sod had been cut at Omaha, and it would not be too long before trains would be running all the way to San Francisco. Carnegie at once wrote a letter to Thomas Scott. Once the nation had made up its mind that its territory would be bound together, there would surely be no time lost in accomplishing it, he said. They should try now to get a contract placing their sleeping cars on the California line.

"Well, young man, you certainly do take time by the forelock," was Scott's reply.

From Rome the four young men went to Naples where they visited still more museums and ancient churches. They climbed Mount Vesuvius, quiet now after a violent eruption six years before that had caused the crater to sink almost two hundred feet. With the energy and high spirits of youth, they hiked the last stage of the climb, to the rim of the crater. The ship that was to take them home already lay at anchor in the Bay of Naples, a reminder that their holiday was drawing to a close. What fun it would be if they could keep on going instead of turning back! They roasted eggs in the hot lava ashes and drank a toast to their return.

The reconciliation between Miller and Phipps failed to take place, despite Carnegie's hopes. At a directors' meeting one day, Miller came into the room and hung up his hat and overcoat. His eyes then fell on Henry Phipps, who had been made a member of the board.

"I refuse to sit at the table with that man!" Miller exclaimed, and grabbed up his hat and coat.

"Come back, Tom, and stop acting like a child," Carnegie pleaded, going up to him. "Come, shake hands with Harry and be friends again."

For answer Tom Miller stalked out the door, slamming it behind him. No amount of persuasion could make him stay in the firm, but he refused to sell his interest to either Kloman or Phipps. He would sell only to Andrew and Tom Carnegie. They paid him something over $70,000, which was above the market value of the time.

Since his return from the walking tour Andrew could not put out of his mind the importance of having sleeping cars on the railway line from Philadelphia to San Francisco. Scott had acted on his advice and made an offer by telegram to the president of the Union Pacific lines, but he had not yet received a reply. Because Carnegie heard that a meeting of the Union Pacific board of directors would be held in New York, he went there to speak to the president in person.

G. M. Pullman from Chicago was a guest at the luxurious St. Nicholas, where Carnegie was also staying. Pullman had been a carpenter, then became a well-known contractor. He had been making sleeping cars and selling them to the railway lines in the Chicago region. Though the Woodruff patent had been taken out first, Carnegie and his partners decided to do nothing about it, for it would have meant years of litigation with probably neither side winning. Carnegie knew now that he and Pullman were in New York for the same reason. He also knew that Pullman was an extraordinary person, one he would rather have as an associate than as a competitor. One evening when Pullman was walking up the marble stairs leading from the hotel lobby, Carnegie joined him.

"Good evening, Mr. Pullman," he said with a friendly smile.

Pullman turned to him in surprise. The two men knew of each other, but were not speaking acquaintances.

"Here we are together, and aren't we making a nice pair of fools of ourselves?" Carnegie went on.

Mr. Pullman drew himself up. "What do you mean, sir?" he demanded.

"Why, by trying to outbid each other as competitors, we are destroying the very advantages we both want."

"Well, what do you propose to do about it?" Pullman asked coldly.

"Unite. We could organize one company, your firm and mine, and make a joint proposition to the Union Pacific."

"And what would you call it?"

"The Pullman Palace Car Company," Carnegie answered.

The man's face relaxed, and he showed signs of being pleased with the idea. It so happened that he had already called on the president of the lines and, after seeing a telegram on his desk to Thomas Scott accepting his proposal, persuaded the man to wait until he too could offer a proposition. By combining with the Woodruff sleeping cars, he would no longer be confined to the western region, but would have his share of cars on the Pennsylvania railroads as far as the east coast as well.

"Come into my room and we'll talk it over," he said.

After the talk they made a joint proposal to the Union Pacific. It was accepted, at a great advantage to both of them.

## CHAPTER VIII   "Thirty-three and an Income of $50,000 per Annum"

The year after the European tour, Andrew Carnegie and his mother moved to New York, where he opened an office on Broad Street. They turned the house at Homewood over to Tom, who had just married Lucy Coleman, one of the five beautiful, vivacious daughters of William Coleman, Andrew's partner in the oil wells. Andrew and his mother had adjoining apartments at the St. Nicholas Hotel. One evening in December, soon after his thirty-third birthday, Andrew Carnegie sat alone in his private parlor, going over his accounts for the year: $15,000 from his bridge company, $20,000 from the Union Iron Mills, $6,000 from the sleeping cars and another $6,000 from the rail mill. The oil stocks were still bringing in large dividends, and there were railroad shares and shares of bank stock besides. He added the column of figures: $56,110.

Sounds from the street below drifted through the closed windows: the clattering of horses' hoofs, the rolling wheels of carriages, and the footsteps going up and down the sidewalk. Twenty years had passed since he landed here, a homesick immigrant boy, and had his first bewildered glimpse of the city from Castle Garden. All that had seemed so far out of reach then was now a part of his life. He was what the world called successful, but had he made the long climb for nothing more than this?

He had seen what greed could do to men. He saw them become ruthless and grasping, manipulating the stock market, corrupting judges and courts, bringing bankruptcy and ruin to any who stood in their way. That kind of life could not bring happiness. He remembered then the ideals of his youth. If the choice had been his, perhaps he would not have become a businessman. He had written letters to the newspapers, dreaming of becoming a writer or an editor. He had practiced public speaking, wanting to be like Uncle Bailie, stirring men to noble thoughts and actions. So that he would not forget his real goal, he put aside his accounts, took a fresh sheet of paper, and commenced to write a set of resolutions for himself:

Thirty-three and an income of $50,000 per annum! By this time two years I can so arrange all my business as to secure at least $50,000 per annum. Beyond this never earn—make no effort to increase fortune, but spend the surplus each year for benevolent purposes. Cast aside business forever, except for others.

Settle in Oxford and get a thorough education, making the acquaintance of literary men—this will take three years' active work—pay especial attention to speaking in public. Settle in London and purchase a controlling interest in some newspaper or live review and give the general management of it attention, taking a part in public matters, especially those connected with education and improvement of the poorer classes.

Man must have an idol—the amassing of wealth is one of the worst species of idolatry—no idol more debasing than the worship of money. Whatever I engage in I must push inordinately; therefore should I be careful to choose the life which will be the most elevating in its character. To continue much longer overwhelmed by business cares and with most of my thoughts wholly upon the way to make more money in the shortest time must degrade me beyond hope of permanent recovery. I will resign business at thirty-five, but during the ensuing two years I wish to spend the afternoons in receiving instruction and in reading systematically.

Three months after writing this, Andrew Carnegie was in London to sell $4,000,000 of first-mortgage bonds for capital to build a bridge across the Mississippi at St. Louis. He called upon the American banker Junius Morgan in his London office and left a printed statement of his plan. The next day when he called, he found Mr. Morgan in an agreeable mood, ready to buy a part of the bonds and take an option on the rest. His lawyers were called in for advice, and they insisted on certain changes in the wording of the bonds.

"You spoke of going to Scotland for a few weeks," Morgan said. "Why not go now? Write to the parties in St. Louis and find out if they agree to the changes. There'll be time enough, when you return, to close the matter."

Carnegie was impatient to close it at once. It would take a letter three weeks to reach St. Louis, and another three weeks to receive an answer. The Atlantic cable had been in use for three years, but only for the headline news of the day. Why couldn't business transactions be sent by cable also? He numbered the printed lines of the bonds and went over each line, making the changes that were wanted, which words to be omitted and which ones added. Before sending the message he showed it to Mr. Morgan.

"Well, young man, if you succeed in that you deserve a red mark," the banker said.

The next morning there was a message from St. Louis waiting for him. "Board meeting last night: changes all approved."

"Now, Mr. Morgan," Carnegie said, showing him the cable, "we can go on with our business if this meets with your lawyers' approval."

Later, at a dinner party, Morgan told the story of the message sent by cable. "That young man will be heard from," he said.

For Carnegie there was an excitement in such a negotiation as this that had little to do with the money. It held a challenge, as any game of competition did, with the risk of losing. But the rules of the game must be fair. He saw what was happening in the New York stock market. Since the end of the war there had been a frenzy of speculation, with the thought of making a fortune in a hurry. Men who could scrape up as much as $500 rushed to a broker to buy shares on margin, hoping for a rise in price. To him it was nothing more than a form of gambling, and often with loaded dice. Too many were losers so that a few could win.

He had his first start, through his friendship with Thomas Scott, buying shares of stock on borrowed money, but he had given it up long ago. He was determined never again to buy what he did not pay for, nor would he sell what he did not own.

After the transaction with Mr. Morgan was closed, An-

drew Carnegie went to Dunfermline. He made a gift of public baths to his native town with a part of his large commis-
sion. He was a Morrison through and through, the relatives
thought, even though he had the fair coloring and happy
disposition of the Carnegies. Thomas Morrison, his grandfather, had once been a successful tanner and leather merchant during the Napoleonic Wars. Uncle Bailie still remembered those days of prosperity when he had a pony of his
own, but the peace after the battle of Waterloo brought ruin
and hard times to the family, and Thomas Morrison went
back to his shoemaking.

Margaret Carnegie had taken a long step from her attic
living quarters on Moody Street to an apartment at the St.
Nicholas Hotel. Five years after the end of the war saw the
beginning of an era of elegance for the North. The St.
Nicholas was the finest hotel in the country, with its fluted
Corinthian columns, its lofty ceilings with frescoes painted
by Italian artists, and hanging chandeliers of sparkling crystal. The walls were hung with rare tapestries and gilt-framed
mirrors, and the floors were covered with carpets of deep
pile. There were times, in spite of this luxury, when Margaret Carnegie missed the simpler life of the past, when her
sons were small and needed all her attention. She was homesick in New York, and missed the relatives and friends in
Pittsburgh more than those in Dunfermline. She eagerly
read the Pittsburgh newspapers, and at every opportunity,
when Andrew made a business trip there, she went along to
stay with Tom and Lucy in the old place at Homewood.

With Andrew it was different. He was not long in making
new friends in New York, with one friendship leading to
another. Alexander King, a fellow Scotsman, and his wife,

Aggie, took him for a New Year's call at the home of John W. Whitfield, a wholesale merchant. Behind the parlor curtains the daughter Louise, a schoolgirl too young to join the group, stood looking on, her blue eyes sparkling as each new guest arrived.

Carnegie was also taken to the home of Mrs. Botta, the former Anne Finch, where he met some of the leading intellectuals of the day. Mrs. Botta was nearly sixty then, white-haired and stately, with the same charm that had attracted such men as Poe, Emerson, Bryant, and Washington Irving. Another group Carnegie especially enjoyed, met once a month, first at the home of Courtney Palmer, then later, when the gathering became too large, at the American Art Gallery. They were called the Nineteenth Century Club, and the members in turn addressed the audience on some leading topic of the day. They were not the kind of people Carnegie associated with in the business world. Instead they shared his interest in literature, music, and in public speaking. A college president was a member of the group, as was a famous literary critic. This was a step in fulfilling his written resolution: "making the acquaintance of literary men . . . pay especial attention to speaking in public." As in the early days at Homewood, he read and studied the subjects to be discussed by the group.

Two years passed, the time he had set for his retirement. Andrew Carnegie could no more stop where he was then than the country itself could have stopped its growth. He made one decision toward that goal, however. When he saw that he had become involved in too many enterprises, he withdrew all his investments from other sources, railroad stock, bank stock, oil wells, to give all his attention to the

manufacture of iron. He did not agree with the old saying
"Don't put all your eggs in one basket." All his good eggs
he'd put in one basket, he said, and he'd keep a careful eye
on that basket.

The Keystone Bridge Company outgrew its first small
shops. New and larger ones were built on ten acres bought
in Lawrenceville. The Union Iron Mills had grown, with
additions made from time to time, so that they had become
the leading mills in the country for making iron parts used
in all kinds of construction.

Sometimes it was not easy for Carnegie to convince his
more conservative partners when he felt they should try
some different method, or embark on a new expansion. No
doubt Kloman muttered to Phipps "I told you so" more than
once. Even his competitors called him foolhardy when he
decided they should build a blast furnace so they could
manufacture their own pig iron. The Lucy Furnace, named
after Tom's young wife, cost twice as much to build as the
estimates given, and there were all the trials and failures the
competitors had predicted and the partners feared. When
they thought they had solved one problem, they found themselves faced with another.

Until then, blast-furnace managers were hired with no
more training for the job than being able to bully the men
under them; as for knowing the condition of the furnaces,
they went by instinct and guesswork. For the Lucy Furnace,
Carnegie chose Henry Curry, a young shipping clerk who
had shown unusual ability and promise. He was one who
could grow as the industry grew.

The next step was to take a chemist into the firm, and
end the guesswork about the quality of ores, limestone, and

coke they used. This was something unheard of, "sheer extravagance" it was called. But when they learned through chemistry that iron stones from some mines with a reputation for quality actually contained less iron than ore from some of the cheaper mines, they discovered that it had been extravagant not to have a chemist in the firm.

"Everything is topsy-turvy," Carnegie said. "The good is bad, and the bad good."

By studying the composition of the ore, they knew what proportion of minerals were needed for fluxing. More iron in the ore meant that less lime was needed. The result was that the Lucy Furnace became so profitable that within two years another furnace was added to it.

Dod Lauder, now a mechanical engineer in Scotland, explained the process of washing and coking the dross from coal mines, as it was done in England. If a superior coke could be made from the waste that was thrown away as useless, Andrew Carnegie wanted to know about it. He had works built along the lines of the Pennsylvania Railroad. Ten-year contracts were drawn with the leading coal companies for their dross, and with the railway companies for transportation. Dod was sent for, and he came to live in Pittsburgh where he was made superintendent of the whole operation.

Another of the Morrison kin had come over from Scotland, and was working as a mechanic in one of the shops, but Carnegie knew nothing about it until one day when the superintendent told him. He met the young man, Tom Morrison, and learned he was the son of his cousin Bob.

"How did you happen to come here?" Carnegie asked.

"I thought we could better ourselves," was the answer.

"We? Who came with you?"

"My wife."

"But why didn't you come to see your relative who might have been able to introduce you here?" Carnegie asked.

"I didn't feel I needed help, if only I got a chance."

There spoke a true Morrison, Carnegie said, taught to depend on himself and asking favors of none. That young man would go far.

He himself had far to go, in spite of the resolutions he had written down. Something was happening to iron as fascinating as it must have been to the man who first discovered the use of the metal. Henry Bessemer, of England, had taken out a patent for making steel by blowing air through molten pig iron. The oxygen of the air combines with most of the impurities of the pig iron. Special compounds were added to remove the excess oxygen and to restore the right amount of carbon and other elements for the grade of steel being made. This method was still in the experimental stage, but Andrew Carnegie knew that if it proved successful, steel would take the place of iron. Certainly in the case of rails, steel would last longer than iron. On certain curves the iron rails had to be replaced every six weeks or two months. He had tried carbonizing the heads of iron rails to make them stronger, and though it worked after a fashion, something better was needed. He had visions of still more uses for steel: in bridges, in construction, in almost everything now made of iron.

He went to England to see a demonstration of this process. A huge container was tilted and molten pig iron poured in. Air was blasted in the bottom and the container turned up. As the silicon and manganese burned out, brilliant

sparks shot through the brown smoke. These turned to
tongues of flame with the burning of the carbon, coloring
the sky blood red. Within fifteen minutes it was all over.

Two rival firms started manufacturing steel by this new
method in Pennsylvania, but Carnegie waited until he felt
the time was right, when it had passed the experimental
stage. Even then his partners, including his brother Tom,
would not join him in the venture. Tom Carnegie shared
his brother's love of books and nature, but he was closer to
his friend Phipps in business affairs. Both were as conservative and cautious as Andrew was daring. As for Kloman,
he was an ironmaster and wanted no part in what he looked
upon as a reckless adventure.

"Then I'll go elsewhere for partners," Andrew Carnegie
said.

He formed his own company, taking in as partners William Coleman, father-in-law of Tom Miller as well as Tom
Carnegie, and David McCandless whose offer of help at
the time of his father's death was still remembered. Edgar
Thomson and Thomas Scott, president and vice-president
of the Pennsylvania Railroad, also became stockholders.

Thomas Scott was building his own railway line, the
Texas Pacific. Carnegie was worried because Scott was doing it mostly on borrowed money. On his return from one
of his trips to Europe, he learned that Scott had reserved
$250,000 interest in the line for him. He paid cash for the
bonds, but he disapproved, and offered advice to his older
friend.

"You can't build thousands of miles of railways until you
get the necessary capital," he said. "Don't build any more
on temporary loans."

Scott refused to listen, but went on borrowing money and went on building. The time came when a large loan fell due in London and there was no money to pay it. Carnegie received a telegram from Scott urging him to come to Philadelphia without fail. He arrived to find several friends, men of affairs, waiting in the office for him. Morgan and Company had agreed to renew the loan if Andrew Carnegie would join the other partners in accepting responsibility.

"No, I can't do that," Carnegie said.

"What! Would you bring ruin to your friends by refusing to stand by them?" he was asked.

It was one of the most trying moments of his life, but he had to refuse. He knew he couldn't pay the Morgan loan in sixty days. He couldn't even pay his proportion as a shareholder. If he could, there would still be other loans that would have to be paid. By accepting responsibility for debts others made, he would risk all that he had built up, and he would also involve his own partners. His brother and his wife, Phipps and his father and sister, Kloman and his family, all would suffer. He owed much to Thomas Scott and he valued their friendship through the years, but there was nothing else he could do.

In September of that year, 1873, he and his mother were still at the summer cottage he had bought in the Allegheny Mountains at Cresson, when news came of the stock-exchange crash. Telegrams began coming in. Jay Cooke and Company, leaders in financing western railway development, failed. E. W. Clarke and Company, another great banking firm of Pennsylvania, failed. One message followed another, with news of the failure of some old established firm. Scott's

Texas Pacific Railway, built with borrowed money, went under.

As if this were not enough, it was discovered that Andrew Kloman had secretly gone in with a group of men to form another iron company on borrowed money. They owed $700,000, which they could not pay, and for Kloman this meant bankruptcy. He had to sell his interests in the Union Iron Mills. Carnegie began to wonder if anything was really sound.

"We'll have to reef sail in every quarter," he said.

Construction was stopped on the new steelworks, and he sold securities he had in reserve. He was not anxious as far as his own business was concerned. Neither he nor his partners had lived extravagantly. None of them had drawn money from the firm to build costly mansions, as men like Gould and Fiske had done. They had not speculated in the stock market, nor had they endorsed the notes of others. With the exception of Kloman, they had not begun new enterprises without enough capital to carry them through. The worries they had were not about debts they owed, but about the money due them. No one was able to pay, and the banks were begging their depositors not to draw upon their balances.

The Keystone Bridge Company, the Union Iron Mills, and the Lucy Furnaces managed to stand firm during the panic and depression. After Kloman had passed through bankruptcy, Carnegie offered to take him back into the firm. As a businessman, Kloman was worse than useless, but no one was equal to him in designing and running new machinery. If he wanted to come back, Carnegie said, he could have a 10 per cent interest. This was less than his former share, but worth $100,000, which could be paid for out of future profits. But there was one condition. He must not go into any other business, nor could he endorse for others. He would have to stay out of business management, and give his whole attention to the mechanics of business. The ambitious Kloman was too proud to accept the offer. He was determined to start a business of his own, with his sons as managers. He was given $40,000 from the firm to make another start, though the new business was doomed to failure from the start.

Work on the steel mill was finished during the year following the panic, and the manufacture of steel rails began. There was the usual search for the right men in the various jobs. Like Curry, manager of the Lucy Furnaces, the new superintendent who took Kloman's place in the Union Iron Mills had started as a shipping clerk. For the steel mill, the manager chosen by Carnegie was Captain Jones, who had once worked as a mechanic at two dollars a day. From the first month of operation, the steel mill was a success. Andrew showed his brother and Henry Phipps the earnings the new company was making, and persuaded them to come in with him. There was no doubt about it, steel would take the place of iron before long, he said. The firm of Carnegie, McCandless and Company then became the Edgar Thomson Steel Company, with Tom and Henry as partners.

# CHAPTER IX   Two
# Americans Abroad

Every boy who goes out to make his way in the world cher-ishes a dream of returning to his native town honored and renowned. Twenty-nine years after Andrew Carnegie left his native home, Dunfermline conferred upon him its highest honor, the freedom of the town. Carnegie saw with pride that on the roll of names there were only two between his and Sir Walter Scott's. He discussed his acceptance speech beforehand with his Uncle Bailie. Though he was always at ease in his talks, and never at a loss for words, the preparation of a public speech never failed to give him some anxiety.

Bailie Morrison had grown old, but there were some traces yet of the fiery radical he had been in his youth. The memory was still in Andrew Carnegie's mind of that night, so long ago, when he was awakened by the whispered news that his uncle had been arrested for making an illegal speech. Thinking of it now as an American, he was sure it was a harmless speech. All that the working people were asking then was the right to vote, and to vote by ballot, the right to run for Parliament, whether they were property owners or not, and equal electoral districts. All these things were taken for granted in the New World.

"I feel like saying what is really in my heart," he said to his uncle.

"Just say that, Andra," the old man replied. "There's nothing like saying what you feel."

A few days later news came from America that a hundred thousand railway workers had gone on strike, holding up the movement of all trains from the Atlantic to the Mississippi. The states called on their militia to break the strike. In Pittsburgh there was a pitched battle between strikers and militiamen. Several men were killed and millions of dollars' worth of property destroyed. Battles were fought in Baltimore, in Columbus, Buffalo, Reading, Chicago, St. Louis, and as far away as the Pacific Coast. Federal troops were sent in, and the strikers had to give up, defeated. Their wages, which were lowered during the panic of 1873, had remained the same, though four years had passed and the country was more prosperous than ever before.

Unlike most of his competitors and partners, Carnegie's sympathies were often on the side of labor. Their right to form trade unions was as sacred as the right of the manufacturer to have his associations and conferences, he believed. But he disapproved of strikes. Labor and capital should be allies, and not enemies, he said. One could not prosper without the other, and their disputes should be solved by arbitration, not by violence.

He could see nothing wrong in the great difference between the income of the laborer and that of the manager.

In his opinion, anyone with enough energy and ambition could climb as high as he wanted. A child born in a dirt-floored cabin grew up to become the country's President. A bobbin boy in a cotton mill now had riches beyond his dreams.

"I should as soon leave my son a curse as the almighty dollar," he wrote in the album of a wealthy woman.

He saw a steady improvement in the workers' condition, since the days when he had his first job, with never a glimpse of daylight during the whole working day. And it would continue to improve.

"All is well since all grows better." Carnegie took up the works of Charles Darwin and Herbert Spencer again, and their philosophy became his. The world as it existed had not been suddenly created. It was the result of a long and gradual process. Neither the world nor man had been created perfect, free from evil and pain. Man had been given the power of advancement. He had risen from the lower to higher forms, and he would go on, his face turned to the light, on his way to perfection.

At forty-three Carnegie had lost none of the enthusiasm for life he had had in his early youth. "Whatever I engage in, I must push inordinately," he had written in his resolution ten years before. He gave himself wholeheartedly to whatever he did, whether in work, in friendship, or recreation. In the fall of 1878 he decided the time had come to fulfill the promise made at the crater of Vesuvius, to go around the world. His many companies, all related to one another, were in good hands and doing well, and he could be spared.

Phipps was too busy, with the boom that followed the

panic, to consider leaving the business, but as for John Vandervort, there was no hesitation. Vandy, who had once said that if he had $1,500 a year, he'd never be caught working like a slave to earn more, was one of the partners now, with thousands coming in every month. This had not changed him. His thoughts were never so concerned with coke or iron or steel that he wouldn't drop it all and go off on an adventure.

In his Broad Street office, Andrew Carnegie closed his desk and locked it.

Vandy joined him in Pittsburgh, and they took the train for San Francisco, following the long trail made by covered wagons such a few years before. The country was vast, and still wild and unsettled over large regions. Two years before, General Custer and his men were massacred by Indians in Montana, and Wild Bill Hickok had been shot dead in the back by a desperado. Buffalo Bill still roamed the plains, and men left the trains to shoot buffalo. The trip across the continent lasted six days, with many stops, and changes from one train to another. On the twenty-fourth of October, the day after their arrival in San Francisco, they boarded the *Belgic,* bound for Japan.

Since his first voyage on the sailboat *Wiscasset,* Andrew Carnegie had crossed the Atlantic so many times that it meant little more to him than the train ride to Pittsburgh. Crossing the Pacific was a new adventure. Instead of the stormy petrel, he saw the albatross. He watched it in its flight, graceful and powerful as it glided overhead, with scarcely a flap of its wings. One evening he saw an albatross swoop down to settle on the water. It was joined by another, and then another, until there were about thirty, huddled together, rocking on the waves all through the night, in the middle of this vast ocean.

There were only twenty-two passengers in first class, but the steerage was crowded with Chinese returning to the place of their birth. They had been brought to this country to build the railroad beds in the western states. Some had grown old, and some were sick. They wanted only to go home to die.

"Another Chinese reported gone today," Carnegie wrote.

He saw the pile of coffins grow larger as the days passed. They were on the wheelhouse, covered with canvas. Not one of the men below would have dreamed of leaving home without being certain that if he should die, his body would be brought back and buried in the same soil as his ancestors. He felt a sympathy with these men. They were like some of the Highlanders of Scotland he had read about. Even a woman who married out of her clan was brought home at her death and buried among her own kin. It was as it should be, he thought. When the race is run, one should return to the place of his beginning.

They were on the ocean twenty-two days. At four o'clock on the fifteenth of November the ship sailed into Yokohama Bay. The sun was setting, and its rays were reflected on snow-covered Mount Fuji in the distance. The mountain seemed suspended in mid-air, with clouds banked around its base, as if they dared rise no higher.

Long after dark the anchor was dropped. Small boats, lighted by flares, crowded alongside to take on passengers. Andrew and Vandy were lowered into one. Four half-naked men stood two on each side, and worked their long oars scull fashion. Each stroke was accompanied with a weird shout such as Western ears had never heard before. At last one of the men, still shouting, began to steer with the oar, as well as scull, and the boat pulled up to the shore. After so long on a rolling ship at sea, the two travelers stepped out with unsteady feet. They followed a runner who lighted the way with a paper lantern, along the narrow streets of Yokohoma, until they reached the hotel. A night watchman passed them, beating on two sticks to announce that all was well.

Twenty-five years ago, no foreigner was allowed to approach this land; and its people, under penalty of death, were forbidden to leave. Crowds gathered about the two Americans wherever they went. Dark, unblinking eyes followed their every movement and gesture. The Americans were as curious about Japan and its people. It was like being in some phantom land, seen only in a dream. They rode in jinrikishas, uncomfortable as other Western men were, at seeing a human being used as a horse. The runners in their enormous domed straw hats were like animated mushrooms bobbing up and down between the shafts. They wore nothing except a thin strip of rag for a loincloth, and flat straw sandals held by straw strings twisted around and between the big toe and the next.

Gay paper lanterns swung over the open shops, and beneath the short curtains over the doorway the shopkeepers and their families could be seen kneeling on raised mat-covered floors, warming their hands over charcoal braziers. Like children dressed up for a game of make-believe, small men and women passed in and out of the shops and along the narrow streets. A man came strutting by, dressed in a dark kimono, walking as if on stilts, in sandals four inches high. Another came half-naked, trotting in bare feet. A baby, riding on its mother's back, was so thickly padded with garment over garment, it was as round as a bear cub. Two men in black silk kimonos met in the middle of the street and bowed. They raised their heads and bowed again. Jinrikishas passed to the side of them, and water carriers and fishmongers moved the bamboo poles across their shoulders to avoid them. They went on bowing with great politeness, but it did not escape Andrew Carnegie that they were taking infinite care each time to lower their heads only the proper number of inches befitting their station. There was a shout of *Huba, huba, huba,* and four men as naked as Adam came by, one at each end of a four-wheel cart, pushing a load of iron.

The two travelers were invited to a banquet where they knelt before small tables on a mat-covered floor. They sat on the floor again at a theater, surrounded by men who ate and smoked and chatted during the day-long performance. Beyond the vermilion gate of a Shinto shrine, they saw a sacred dance. Three old priests sat on a stage. One beat a small hand drum, one played a bamboo flute, and one fingered a banjo-like samisen. A beautiful young priestess stepped out, dressed in robes of white and orange, and danced with slow and stately movements in time to the music. It was a prayer in motion, felt by those who witnessed it.

In a temple garden a woman, neatly but not richly dressed, knelt before a statue of one of the gods. She was young, but her blackened teeth showed her to be a married woman. She prayed so long and so earnestly that she was not aware of the presence of the two foreigners. There was no mistaking her sincere devotion. Her very soul was lifted up to some power considered higher than herself, Andrew Carnegie said. He wondered what sorrow could so move her. He asked the interpreter, after they were beyond hear ing distance of the woman. She was praying for one thing the interpreter answered, the old prayer that a man child be born to her.

"Suppose it is not answered?" Carnegie asked.

"She will be sent away from her husband's household and another brought in to take her place," was the answer

Carnegie walked away saddened at the thought that all a woman holds dear, should be trembling thus in the balance

One night when he and Vandy were in the hotel room to gether, he sat at a table, writing in his journal. Suddenly he felt the chair shake as if someone were trying to pull it from under him. He looked up to see Vandy standing in amaze ment, trying to keep his balance while the floor rocked to and fro. It was an earthquake, the first of many they were to experience in Japan, and it gave them a strange, helpless feeling.

For the rest of the trip, Carnegie and Vandervort no longer found themselves the objects of a childlike curiosity stared at and followed, as they had been in Japan. The British had moved into the Chinese cities the two travelers now visited. Hong Kong was a British Crown Colony, and India was part of the Empire upon which the sun never set.

In Hong Kong on Christmas morning, at eight o'clock, they went to the English Cathedral to hear a performance of the "Hallelujah Chorus." Japanese and Chinese music was discordant to Carnegie's ears, and he longed to hear organ music again. Outside the church were about fifty or

ixty sedan chairs, each with a number of coolies dressed in
orgeous livery. Some of the men were gambling; some
tretched out in the shade, waiting for their British employ-
rs to come out after the services were over. Many of the
vorshipers inside were Scotsmen, Carnegie noticed, stern in
heir attitude toward the Sabbath, yet they thought nothing
f keeping so many human beings on duty simply to save
hemselves from walking a few short squares to church. But
vas this worse, after all, he asked himself, than riding in
ne's carriage with coachman and footman to the Fifth
Avenue churches in New York? That hadn't struck him as
nything out of the way until then. After this, he declared,
inless the future Mrs. Carnegie, whoever she might be, had
erious objections, they should walk to church when they
vent.

On New Year's Eve, aboard the ship *Pie Ho,* he wrote
lown his resolution for the coming year: "See what you
re good for."

He had seen poverty in the Orient worse than anything
e could imagine. The poverty of his childhood, and the
overty even now in the slums of big cities in America, were
f a different kind, for with them there was hope. An under-
aid hod carrier or section hand on a railroad could dream
f a better life ahead, if not for himself, for his sons and
laughters. In Asia there was only a resigned hopelessness.
t had been bad in Japan and China and the Crown Col-
nies, but India was far worse.

It was in February, the dry season, when the two reached
ndia. The landscape was one vast scorched plain. Dust
ettled over everything; the little mud hovels with roofs of
traw, the scanty clothes the people wore, even the sky it-

self took on the same muddy color of the earth. There ha
been squalor in Shanghai, but there at least there was n
dust, and the people wore more clothes.

India was still suffering from the effects of the famin
of 1876 and 1877. Over five million people had died c
starvation or disease as a result of those two terrible year
That was more than the whole population of Scotland, Ca
negie mused. He remembered that it was during this tim
that the most gorgeous reception ever held in India was o
dered to gratify the whim of Queen Victoria when she wa
made Empress of India.

"Perhaps the poor Queen didn't know about the famine,
he wrote. "Her books show that her interest in life was con
fined strictly to the petty details of her household, and na
row circle of satellites."

He wished England's hands were free from stain in con
nection with the opium grown in India. China should not b
forced by England to buy a drug so pernicious. Whateve
benefits England or any other country bestowed upon an
other race were more than canceled by the evil of interfer
ence. When even the most underdeveloped of nations wa
robbed of self-government, when responsibility was take
away from them—and interference, he said, did take it awa
—that meant the end of natural growth for the nation.

"Rob them of the freedom to act, to accept, to reject," h
wrote in his journal, "and all that England can give in retur
will not atone for the injury she inflicts. A nation shoul
have much to offer in exchange, more than I can see an
nation has, which stifles in the breast of the most ignorar
people in the world the sacred germ of self-development.

The blame for India's tragedy he found not England'

alone. Long before the British came to this country, the degrading caste system was in existence. Throughout India he saw many miserable, wretched human beings, mere skeletons, sitting or lying beside dusty roadsides, the only home they knew, rousing themselves only to beg a pittance from passers-by. The masses were always on the brink of starvation. A little too much rain, or too little, and millions of lives were threatened. He saw also the splendor and luxury in the lives of the upper classes. The wealth of an Indian prince in gold and jewels was greater than the wealth of any American capitalist.

It was strange, Carnegie thought, that the caste system should exist in the country that saw the birth of the compassionate Buddha. Then he reminded himself that warring Christian nations founded their system on the teachings of the Prince of Peace.

There was beauty in India, along with injustice, inequality, and poverty, a beauty never to be forgotten. Andrew Carnegie was to remember for the rest of his life a caged tiger he saw in Madras, caught only a short while before. Compared with tigers he had seen in zoos, it was magnificent. The coat was a fiery brown with black stripes as glossy as leather. The wild burning eyes, like topazes set in its head, stared at him an instant, then, with a savage roar, it gave one leap from the back of the cage, shaking the bars until they rattled like reeds.

He had heard of the beauty of the Taj Mahal. Stern men had become so overpowered by the sight of it, they burst into tears, it was said. Carnegie and Vandervort went there by carriage, their minds made up that they would be disappointed. No place could live up to such a reputation as

that. It was late afternoon when they arrived, and after th
first glance the two friends quietly parted, each to go hi
own way, alone with his thoughts.

"There are some objects too sacred for analysis, or eve
for words," Carnegie wrote later. "And I know now ther
is a human structure so exquisitely fine and unearthly, as t
lift it into this holy domain."

He wandered about, looking from every side, in a moo
of melancholy and at the same time solemnly elated. As th
sun was setting, he sat down in the garden in full view o
the Taj. Before long an Englishman approached, and wit
a slight nod, sat down quietly without speaking a word
There was something of reverence that showed in his face
When he spoke, it was as if he were talking to himself.

"I stayed away from this, in England, as long as I could
It is seven years since I was here before. This time I've bee
here for two weeks, wandering about the grounds. I mus
tear myself away tomorrow, and my grief is that I canno
take a perfect image of this with me. I may have to retur
again."

"My feeling is the opposite," Carnegie said. "The imag
of this will never leave me."

"I envy you," the Englishman replied.

The sun set, and it began to grow dark. Andrew left to g
in search of Vandy. He found him in the archway, gazin
before him as if under a spell.

"I should have looked you up earlier, but I couldn't brin
myself to leave this spot," he said.

Andrew nodded sympathetically. Till the day he died, h
said, wherever he was and whenever the mood came ove
him of all that was most sacred, most elevated, most pure

there would be his memory of the lovely charm of the Taj Mahal.

From India the two companions went to Egypt, but by then they had grown weary of strange sights and sounds and places. In Egypt everything was as they expected: Cairo with its commanding citadel, its hundreds of mosques with their slender spires and minarets, the impressive Pyramids standing aloof in the desert, the Sphinx, mysterious, telling of no human passion yet seeming to tell of all, the end of all. All these were so familiar it was as if they had seen them sometime before. Even the misery and poverty no longer appalled them, so familiar were they by now with crowds of squalid wretches surrounding them, clamoring for money, the mud hovels where they managed to live, the coarse food they ate, and the greasy, unwashed rags that hung loosely upon them. Could one grow indifferent when this was constantly before him?

Carnegie thought of the workers in these countries, doomed to a life of unremitting toil, from morning till night, every day in the week. Their festival and fête days, coming at long, irregular intervals, were no substitute for the one day in the week, of rest. He compared these workers with a worker of Europe or America. One day out of seven, he puts on his best clothes, his wife gives the cottage an extra cleaning, and something special is prepared for dinner. The day is marked by a hundred little differences from those of labor, a stroll in the fields, a visit to relatives, a meeting with neighbors in church. These things, he said, lie close to the root of all improvement.

He and Vandy decided not to go to Greece and Turkey as they had planned. They would go on to Italy from Egypt, and save those countries for another time, when they could look with fresh eyes.

Five months after sailing out of the Golden Gate at San Francisco, they were in Naples, with the view of Mount Vesuvius before them. They couldn't stand at the crater now to roast eggs and drink a toast, for the volcano was in eruption. Puffs of white steam rose up to float in the cloudless Italian sky. The two friends shook hands and remembered the pledge made years ago. Now it was fulfilled, and the time had come for another toast. May life hold for them another such five months of glorious adventure.

In Naples Carnegie learned about a young English chemist, Sidney Thomas, who had found a way to rid iron ore of phosphorus, that enemy of good steel, by uniting it with some other chemical in the smelting. If this could be done successfully, it would solve the worst of the problems in steelmaking.

In France, he made an excursion from Paris to a famous iron and steel works. The size of it was staggering. The rolling mill alone was 1,500 by 350 feet. Masses of steel weighing as much as 30 tons were handled as easily as his own mills handled a rail ingot. Here he was shown one ingot of steel that weighed 120 tons. This monstrous machinery made only war matériel. Steel for peaceful industry was made with ordinary machinery.

"May it be long before America can boast of an engine half this size," Andrew Carnegie wrote in his journal that night.

In England he attended a meeting of the British Iron and Steel Institute. He was impressed with the thoroughness that went into their manufacture of iron and steel, and their sci entific knowledge of it. There were no trade secrets here, and Carnegie wished that in America there could be such a free exchange of theory and practice.

His mother had come to London to meet him, and together they went to Scotland. After a short visit there, they sailed for New York. Eight months had passed since he had left it. Looking back over his trip, Carnegie felt it had been well worth while. It had brought him a clearer sense of the brotherhood of man and the unity of race. He had found good in all the countries, and evil too. Men did not differ in their trials and sufferings, or in their triumphs and rejoicings. Again the words of Robert Burns came to him as he wrote in the last page of his notebook:

> Then let us pray that come it may,
>     As come it will for a' that;
> That sense and worth, o'er a' the earth,
>     May bear the gree, and a' that:
>         For a' that, and a' that,
>             It's coming yet, for a' that,
>         That man to man, the warld o'er,
>             Shall brothers be for a' that.

From New York, Carnegie went on to Pittsburgh with Vandervort, back to the mills and factories that were part of his life. But there was something here that neither he nor Vandy had noticed before. Of all the races they had seen, the Americans were the saddest-looking. Life was so terribly earnest here, and the people knew no real rest. There seemed to be one thought in the minds of all, from the man who handled the spade to the man who employed thousands. That was to get ahead. Perhaps, after all, the workers in those older lands, robbed of ambition as they were, stopped oftener to rest, and found more enjoyment out of what life offered them.

John Vandervort, who had never been happy in the business world, was soon to retire, so he could have more time for the things he enjoyed. The old wish to do the same came back to Andrew Carnegie. Among life's saddest spectacles, he said, was that of an elderly man occupying his last years of life grasping for more dollars. But forty-three was not elderly. And about that method of extracting phosphorus from ironstone. There was something well worth looking into.

# CHAPTER X  A Library for Dunfermline

When the owner of the St. Nicholas Hotel built a new and more elegant one, the Windsor, at Fifth Avenue and Forty-sixth Street, Andrew Carnegie and his mother made that their home. Margaret Carnegie had grown so accustomed by now to a life of luxury that she no longer wanted to take on the responsibility of a home. She had her own personal maid and a coachman to drive her carriage. Sometimes when she was lonesome she rode down to her son's office on Broad Street and walked in unannounced, whether he was busy or not. Once when Carnegie was alone in his private office, bent over his desk, hard at work, he saw her enter. He kept on quietly with what he was doing, as if she were not there. He could hear her footsteps moving about the room, pausing when she picked up something and put it down again, then going on to something else.

After about a half hour of this, she spoke, in her broad Scotch accent, "I'll be going now; I only came in to bother ye."

Andrew laughed as he got up and took her arm, guiding her to the door. "Yes, Mother," he said, "but you didn't succeed."

Never had a woman a more devoted son, but there were some parts of his life from which she was excluded. Every day, in fair weather, he could be seen riding one of his horses along the bridle trails of Central Park. Often there was a woman companion with him. Margaret Carnegie had seen many of them come and go: society women, famous actresses, opera stars.

"There's no woman good enough to marry my Andra," she was heard to say more than once.

On the first day of 1880, the year after his return from the trip around the world, Andrew Carnegie went out to pay his New Year's calls. Again he went with his friends Alexander and Aggie King to the Whitfield home. Mr. Whitfield had died since he was there last, and Louise, the schoolgirl who had looked on from behind the parlor curtains, was now a young lady of almost twenty-three, gracious and poised as she assisted her mother as hostess.

"She's very fond of riding," King said to Carnegie later, and suggested that he invite her to ride with him.

Louise Whitfield asked her mother's permission before she accepted the invitation. Her long black riding habit had been made by the family dressmaker, and with it she wore a tall hat and smart kid gloves. She was slender and graceful riding sidesaddle beside this man of the world almost twice her age. Louise Whitfield decided, on that first ride, that whatever the future might hold for her, this would always remain the great experience of her life. There were other rides to follow. Often after that the two could be seen, sometimes cantering, and sometimes at a slow trot, absorbed in quiet talk.

Andrew Carnegie enjoyed the company of attractive women. Of the two brothers, Tom was the family man, delighting in his home, his wife, Lucy, and their nine children. Andrew enjoyed his bachelorhood. Once he had made a promise to his mother that he would not marry during her lifetime, and so far he had not found that promise hard to keep.

Louise Whitfield was at first only one of the many young women he rode with in the park, but as the months passed, his thoughts turned more and more to her. When he invited friends to share his box at the opera with his mother and himself, she was often included. He took her to the concert, with his mother often going along as well. Once when he and Louise went for a ride in the park, Margaret Carnegie called on Mrs. Whitfield and took her and the two younger children, Harry and Stella, for a drive in her carriage.

If there were times when Carnegie felt the difference in their ages was too great, Miss Whitfield knew that with her it did not matter. She was very much in love. Andrew gave her a copy of one of the popular books of that year, Sir Edwin Arnold's *Light of Asia*, and he read passages of it aloud to her.

"I always carry the *Light of Asia* around with me every place I go," Louise wrote to Carnegie when he had gone to Scotland for the summer. "I love to pick it up, even if only to read but a few lines, and it always refreshes me and does me good. I wish I had it, as you have, at my tongue's end, but I have committed a few of the loveliest bits to memory."

She spent that summer at the family home in the Catskill

Mountains, and it was not until winter that she and Andrew met again. He still had his summer home at Cresson Springs in Pennsylvania, in the Alleghenys, where he and his mother always went after returning from abroad.

Andrew Carnegie had made a gift of a public library to his home town that summer, and he had been asked to take part in the ceremony of laying the cornerstone the following year. He began making plans to take a group of friends on a coaching trip with his mother and himself, from Brighton to Inverness.

The idea for a coaching trip through Britain had first come to him when he, Phipps, and Vandervort made their walking tour fifteen years ago. He had said then that someday, when his ship came home, he would drive a party of his closest friends all the way from Brighton to Inverness. He had been reminded of this by a book he had read, *The Strange Adventures of a Phaeton,* describing just such a journey by the author, William Black. His ship had come home now, and his list of friends had grown so that it was not easy to limit the invitations.

Miss Whitfield was invited, and wanted desperately to go, but her mother felt it was not proper for a young, unmarried girl to go on such an excursion, and would not give her consent. Louise Whitfield pleaded. Their friends the Alexander Kings would be in the group, and certainly Mrs. Carnegie herself would be chaperone enough. Mrs. Whitfield remained firm in spite of her daughter's arguments.

Carnegie thought that perhaps his mother might influence Mrs. Whitfield to change her mind, and he asked her to try. Margaret Carnegie did as her son asked. She ordered her carriage and was driven to the Whitfield home, where she was received in the drawing room. There she extended an invitation as formally as her Scotch accent could make it. Louise was disappointed that she did not urge further when Mrs. Whitfield said she regretted, but must decline on behalf of her daughter. Instead, Mrs. Carnegie agreed with the mother. She pointed out the inconveniences of a single girl of twenty-three going off on such a trip, stopping overnight at inns along the way.

"If she were a daughter of mine, she wouldn'a go," she said, as she took her leave.

A week before he was to sail, Carnegie was in Washington, where he dined with the newly elected President Garfield at the home of his friend Secretary Blaine. After dinner, when the ladies retired to the drawing room, the gentlemen lingered over their wine and cigars. The talk turned to the coming coaching trip.

"It sounds like Black's *Adventures of a Phaeton* on a grand scale," Garfield said.

They talked about the author and other books he had written.

"I am provoked with Black just now," Garfield went on. "A man who writes to entertain has no right to end a story as miserably as he ended *Macleod of Dare*. Fiction should give us the bright side of existence. Real life has tragedies enough of its own."

It seemed to Carnegie that he saw a sad, careworn expression on the President's face as he spoke. Perhaps his thoughts were on the assassination of Czar Alexander II of Russia that had happened at the time of his own inauguration, in March.

The nine guests of the coaching party met in New York.

Henry Phipps, now married, was there with his wife. David McCargo was one of the guests. In all, there were five women and six men, including Andrew and his mother. Carnegie called for Louise Whitfield and took her to dine with the group at the Windsor Hotel the evening before sailing. She sat quietly through the dinner, scarcely able to hide her disappointment as the other guests talked about the coming trip.

Andrew Carnegie was at his happiest planning and organizing, and in this adventure he spared no details. He had ordered the coach in advance, and it was ready when the ship landed, with coachman and footman. He awoke early in his room at the Grand Hotel at Brighton. When he pulled up the heavy Venetian blinds, he could look out on the sea with its hundreds of pretty little sails. The day was fair, a good omen for the start of the trip. The coach, new, and as glossy as a mirror, was driven up to the hotel door. The horses, four handsome bays, their harness and buckles glistening in the sun, were champing at the bit, impatient to be on the way. A large crowd had gathered to see them off, some friends and some curiosity seekers.

Margaret Carnegie had the seat of honor next to the coachman, Perry. Aggie King sat beside her, and the rest of the group found their places, each carrying a small handbag and a strap package with raincoat, walking shoes and shawl, prepared for any kind of weather. The trunks would be forwarded every week to their Saturday destination so there could be a change of clothes. They would not travel on Sundays, and, to make a difference between that day and the others, they would wear full dress for dinner.

When all was ready, the footman, Joe, stepped up behind

and, with a blast of the horn, the coach was off through the streets of Brighton and up the hills toward Guilford, forty-two miles away.

"Skid, Joe," said the coachman.

"Right, Perry," said the footman.

Someone in the group began to sing, and the others joined in:

> "The present moment is our ain,
> The neist we never see—"

As they rode north, they had perpetual summer with them. In cottage gardens and along the roadside foxgloves, buttercups, and daisies were in bloom, and the bluebells were at their most beautiful. There were picnic lunches on the banks of a stream or under a shade tree in some clover-covered field. Joe and Perry took out the two food hampers and emptied them. The larger one, turned on end, served as a table, and the smaller one was a seat for Mrs. Carnegie. They spread rugs on the ground for the others in the group. Sometimes they went to the nearest inn and brought back mugs of ale, Devonshire cider, or pitchers of fresh, creamy milk.

Several of the guests left the luncheon ground early, to walk until the coach could overtake them, or they dismounted before reaching the end of the journey and walked to the village where they were to stay the night. The ladies gathered wildflowers along the hedgerows, and the men wore a flower for a boutonniere.

Once on such a stroll Andrew Carnegie and some of his companions stopped at a country inn for a cup of tea. It was a poor little place, with benches instead of chairs around the table, but the tile floor was spotlessly sanded, and roses bloomed beside the door. The landlady said that her husband was working as gardener for the squire. They had come to this place only recently from one of the Midland towns, for their children's health. The two little daughters, pale and blonde, came shyly into the room. Carnegie made friends with them and put a few pence in their hands. The older, no more than six years old, went to the next room and brought back a sheet of paper with some penny postage stamps pasted on it.

"The girls will buy stamps with the money you've given them," their mother said.

She explained that the Post Office Department allowed 2½ per cent interest, and the squire had said that if a child on his property saved eleven stamps, he'd give the twelfth, to make it a shilling. What a pity, Carnegie thought, that children so young had to learn that life was a constant struggle for subsistence. Though he had had to learn it in his own childhood, he felt that civilization was a failure until this was changed.

The coach drove up to take his companions and him on. His thoughts kept going back to the two little girls with their pale, serious faces.

"Why didn't we give them a shilling each, with strict orders that they spend it to gorge themselves on taffy and gingerbread, and not save a penny?" he said.

"Oh, it would have made them sick," someone spoke up.

"Well, what if it did! Think of the memory they'd have. That sweet taste would linger in their mouths till they were grown. Wouldn't that be worth a little sickness?"

Margaret Carnegie celebrated her seventy-first birthday

in Windsor, two days after they left Brighton. It was Sunday, their first day of rest. At breakfast the guests presented her with a silver cup ornamented with birds and flowers, and inscribed with her name. Andrew was as surprised as his mother. He stood up to make an acceptance speech, but she motioned him to sit down. She would make her own speech of thanks.

They went to church after breakfast, where they saw the Prince of Wales come up the aisle. Gladstone, the Prime Minister, followed at a respectful distance and took his place several pews behind. Carnegie looked at his pensive, noble face and thought he was worth a dozen men like the Prince of Wales. "As noble as any Prince in the realm," he said.

Later in the day Sidney Thomas, the young chemist, arrived with his sister, from London. A pale Gladstonian youth and one of the truly great men of the time, Carnegie described him. They were invited to stay for the evening meal. Phipps as well as Carnegie had many questions to ask about the discovery he made with his cousin Gilchrist, that phosphorus had a greater affinity for lime than for iron. By using lime in the process, with heat not under 2,500 degrees, the phosphorus could be drawn off from the slag that floated to the top. The toy pot the two chemists used for their first experiment was compared to Watts's teakettle proving the power of steam.

The days were never boring, no matter how long the drive. They sang, they drowsed, and they got out to walk beside the coach. There were long discussions on serious matters, or on such trivial things as when a woman was at her loveliest. There were harmless flirtations between the young ladies and the single men in the group. The ladies gave coquettish answers, with coy glances toward the men. A woman was most attractive when riding horseback, Andrew Carnegie declared.

The mother decided she was missing too much in her place of honor beside the coachman. She insisted on changing her place for one in the middle of the back form, where she could hear what everybody was saying. She also had an audience for her own stories and ballads. "Her tongue went from morning till night," her son observed. Once after lunch she and Aggie King went wading in the brook; when they came out on the green field, they kilted their skirts and danced a Highland reel.

On the fourth morning after leaving Brighton, Andrew Carnegie sat in his room at the hotel in Reading, and wrote his first letter to Miss Whitfield while waiting for his friends to assemble. It was not a letter to bring much comfort to the disappointed young woman, who must have been waiting eagerly for some news from him. He addressed her as "Well My Dear Friend." He had waited to write until he could say whether the Gay Charioteers were a success or not. It was all as he had pictured it, and more. The days were perfect; everyone was so happy, that it was almost too much like paradise. "But Oh My Friend! would you were with us," he wrote. Then, as if he had said too much, he wrote about the ideal weather: no rain except a few drops at night, enough to lay the dust. He hoped she would enjoy her summer, gave his regards to her mother, and ended with "Goodbye, Your friend, A. Carnegie."

The second day of July was on a Sunday, another day of rest. Their trunks were waiting for them at the Izaak Walton

Inn at Dovedale, and the fresh clothes were unpacked. They
had planned to have a gay celebration on the Fourth, with
firecrackers and American flags, and perhaps a few patriotic
speeches. On Monday they were gaily on their way to the
next destination when they were shown a copy of the London *Times*. The President of the United States had been shot
on the second of July.

There was a mood of depression over the group, including even the coachman and footman. Carnegie recalled his
last meeting with President Garfield, and his sad, careworn
expression as he said, "Real life has tragedies enough of its
own." The plans for the Fourth of July celebration were
dropped. No one cared to gather wildflowers on the way-
side, and there were no songs for the first time since they
started. To each it was as if some member of the family,
dearly loved, had died. How could it be possible that a man,
exuberantly alive one minute, walking in a railway station
to meet his wife, should the next minute lie close to death.
A disgruntled office seeker, who in his warped mind imagined himself wronged, had shot him. There was some comfort in the thought that the shot had not killed him instantly.
He was still alive, and there was still hope.

Day by day the news in the London *Times* was more encouraging, and spirits began to lift. At one stop Andrew
Carnegie had such confidence in the President's recovery
that he sent a telegram of congratulations to Blaine, the
Secretary of State.

Andrew Martin, the son of the old schoolmaster at Dunfermline, now an officer in the Queen's Volunteer Army,
joined the party as they drew near Scotland, and rode the
rest of the way with them. His train came in that night at

eleven, but, late as it was, he was made to sing a Scotch song to prove he was one of them.

The schoolmaster's son, brought up on his father's maxim, "You have not been put into this world to enjoy yourselves but to do your duty," was at first a little overwhelmed by the exuberant group of Scotch Americans. With a somber expression he began to sing in the broad accent of his country:

> "See yonder paukie shepherd
> Wha' lingers on the hill.
> His ewes are in the fauld,
> And his sheep are lying still."

He lowered his voice and softly sang the last stanza:

> "But he downa gang to rest,
> For his heart is in a flame
> To meet his bonnie lassie
> When the kye come hame."

The group applauded and acclaimed him as truly one of them. Before long, in spite of his stern Scotch upbringing, he joined in the spirit of fun. As they drew near the border, they saw the thistle and harebells blooming, and the heather was in all its beauty. Young Martin got out to walk with the others, and stopped when they did to gather wildflowers along the hedgerows.

"Mon," he exclaimed, "this canna be a *verra* bad thing we're doing!"

David McCargo sang "Cowden Knowes," and Martin listened in astonishment.

"Whaur did ye get that?" he asked. "Ye didna get that song out of a book."

"Right," Carnegie agreed. "The only place to get a Scotch song is at your father's knees."

McCargo was born an American, but his father was as Scotch as William Carnegie. He shared the excitement of the group when they came to the border, and had the same feeling of homecoming when he stepped his foot on Scottish soil at Gretna Green. A little Scots lad came up when he saw the group and offered to act as their guide. He said his name was Davie. Carnegie gave him a shilling.

"Do you know Burns?" he asked the boy.

"Aye. I ken 'A mon's a mon for a' that' and 'Auld Lang Syne,' " was the reply.

"Good for you, Davie. Here's another shilling. Now, if you can't remember anything else, let it be 'A man's a man for a' that.' Scotsmen will need to remember that one of these days when we set things right. And don't forget 'Auld Lang Syne' either."

"What is your address, sir?" the boy asked. "When I grow up to be a man, maybe I'll go to America."

"Do that," Carnegie said, giving the boy his address. "I'll help you get your start, provided you haven't forgotten Robert Burns."

When the coach drove on, he added, "We may make a Republican out of him yet, and have him return to preach the equality of man, the sermon Scotland needs."

The air now was sweet with the smell of honeysuckles in the hedgerows. Above them long, graceful sprays of the wild rose were in full bloom. A startled pheasant or partridge flew off at their approach, with a whirr of its wings, and the cawing of rooks could be heard in the distance. The glens were carpeted with Scottish bluebells. The coach could make little progress with the commands often given:

"Stop, Perry!"

"Right, sir."

"Steps, Joey!"

"Right, sir."

Margaret Carnegie ranged the sides of the glen, with no thought of time. The horn sounded for her, and still she lingered, to emerge at last with her arms full of flowers.

Andrew Martin was reminded of a song by a man from Dunfermline who had gone to India:

"The palm tree waveth high, and fair the myrtle springs,
And to the Indian maid the bulbul sweetly sings,
But I dinna see the broom wi' its tassels on the lea,
Nor hear the linties sing o' my ain countree."

When they approached Edinburgh they could look down from a hilltop and see the sparkling Firth of Forth. Beyond lay Dunfermline. "That auld gray toon I love," Carnegie called it. A member of the Dunfermline council called on him in Edinburgh and hinted that the town was planning a great reception for him. Later a telegram came asking if he would postpone his coming for a day. He began to have some misgivings about what was in store for him, and thought about the speech he must make.

"I won't do all the suffering," he said at dinner that night. "You men are in for it too."

The men pleaded with the ladies to vote they'd be excused.

"Why, your speeches are bound to be hits. A man's first speech always causes a sensation," Carnegie said.

He had hoped for a fair day to go to Dunfermline, and

his hope was more than realized. Morning dawned as bright and magnificent as that morning, fifty days ago, when they had left Brighton.

From the top of Ferry Hill they caught a glimpse of the town. How beautiful it looked from here, with the grand old Abbey towering over all, giving charm and dignity even to the humblest tenement! But where were the people? The place looked as dead as on a Sabbath day.

He was soon to learn that everybody had gone to the city line to welcome him. A triumphal arch had been raised at the entrance to the town. The town officials were dressed in the full regalia of their office, but the man chosen to give the speech of welcome was a workman, a representative of the Weavers' Guild. Andrew Carnegie was deeply moved by this tribute to his weaver father, and by the simple eloquence of the speech itself.

The town band played "The Star-Spangled Banner," and a procession almost a mile long escorted the coach and its occupants through the town. Women and girls from the linen factories, dressed in white, marched in the parade. There were also weavers and dyers, carpenters and masons, gardeners, foresters, bakers, and foundry men. The streets were hung with flags; banners were stretched from one side to the other with the words "Welcome Carnegie"; and almost every house was decorated with colored bunting draped over doors or windows. All stores and factories were closed, and everyone was dressed in Sunday clothes.

The procession passed the well at the head of Moody Street where a small boy once dreamed great dreams. They passed the shop where Margaret had sold cabbages and sweets. They stopped briefly at the house where Andrew was born, and there was a silence; then they started on again. An American flag was waving from the Abbey tower. It was the first time in all the long history of the Abbey that a foreign flag had been raised. As they rode along the Pends, the sweet bells began to toll. This was too much for Andrew. He no longer tried to hold back the tears. The world could have no higher honor for him than the sound of the Abbey bells welcoming him and his mother back to Dunfermline.

He had been asked to lay the cornerstone for the new library, but he wanted this honor to go to his mother. On the day of the ceremony, Margaret Carnegie, dressed in black silk, with a small black bonnet over her white hair, held the silver trowel in her work-worn hands that had performed much harder labor than this. She spread the mortar with the trowel, then gave the rock three taps, and announced, "I pronounce this stone duly and properly laid, and may God bless this undertaking." She was then given the silver trowel as a memento.

The architect who drew the plans for the library building, Carnegie's gift to his home town, had asked him about his family coat of arms, which he wanted to have carved over the entrance door.

"I have no coat of arms," Carnegie had replied. "Above the door carve instead, 'Let there be light.' "

Just so had there been light for him on that day he borrowed his first book from Colonel Anderson's library.

On the last day of the journey, just before reaching Inverness, several of the group left the coach to walk the rest of the way. It was here that Macbeth had his castle which the good King Duncan visited, and where he was murdered. As if reflecting the mood of the party, the wind blew mournfully over the moors with such force that the hikers had to take refuge in a schoolhouse until the coach could catch up with them. They sang their last song together that night after dinner:

> "Happy we've been a' togither,
> Happy we've been ane and a'.
> Blyther folk ne'er coached togither.
> Sad are we to gang awa'."

The words "good night and happy dreams" were spoken with unusual tenderness at bedtime. The seven weeks of carefree holiday had come to an end.

In New York they learned the news that James Garfield, after such a gallant struggle for life, had had a relapse. Less than a month later he was dead, and Chester Arthur became the new President.

One of the coaching party, Benjamin Vandervort, had stayed on with the Carnegies in New York after their return to the St. Nicholas Hotel. But before long he, too, was gone.

"All our family is gone," Carnegie said to his mother. "I feel so lonely, so deserted."

"Oh, you don't count me, then," said the mother. "You still have one who sticks to you."

He replied with a teasing rhyme:

> "The good book tells of one
> Who sticks closer than a brother.
> But who would dare to say there's one
> Sticks closer than a mother?"

# CHAPTER XI  Author, Bridegroom, Philanthropist

One stormy day in the winter that followed, Andrew Carnegie looked out the window of his room. It seemed scarcely worth while to venture out in such weather, especially since his office was at least three miles from the hotel where he lived. He picked up the notes he had made on the coaching trip the past summer, and began reading them to pass the time. They might be made into a magazine article, he thought, and he began to put down a few lines to see how they went. He became so absorbed in it that before the day was over he found he had written between three and four thousand words, and still he had hardly begun. He saw that it was growing too long for a magazine article, but it could be made into a book that he would have printed in a private edition of a few hundred copies to give to his friends.

Every stormy day after that, when there was no urgent need to go to his office, he spent the time at his desk, writing and living over each day of that glorious summer. He could hear again the chime of the Abbey bell tolling its welcome to him. The world had not in its power to devise, much less to bestow, such a reward as that which the Abbey bell gave when it tolled in their honor, he said.

"Rousseau wished to die to the strains of sweet music. Could I choose my accompaniment, I could wish to pass into the dim beyond with the tolling of the Abbey bell sounding in my ears, telling me of the race that had been run, and calling me, as it had called the little white-haired child, for the last time—to sleep."

Mr. Scribner, whose publishing firm printed the private edition, read the book and liked it well enough to want to publish it on a royalty basis. He brought it out in 1882 and gave it the title *An American Four-in-Hand in Britain*. The first edition of two thousand was immediately sold, and the book went into several more editions, and was published in England as well. The joy of becoming a professional author meant more to Carnegie, perhaps, than any business transaction he had made.

"Everybody is talking about your book, *An American Four-in-Hand in Britain*," Louise Whitfield wrote to him when he was in Scotland that summer. "I have cut out some very flattering criticisms from the different papers which I will some day show you. We are all proud of you and love to think that you are our friend."

He had been seeing Miss Whitfield often during the past winter. Her home was a short walking distance from the Windsor Hotel. Sometimes there were long drives in buckboard or surrey out beyond the city. They went to concerts together, and to lectures, to the theater or opera. There was an exchange of letters when Andrew was away from New York. Hers, though she addressed him as "My Dear Mr.

Carnegie," were warm, with gentle hints of tenderness that tried to reach him.

"Oh how glad your letter made me for I was really afraid this year you would forget all about writing. But you didn't forget after all, and so made a certain individual very happy. I carried it off all by myself, to the loveliest little nook in the woods, and had a good time reading of all your gay doings—"

Carnegie's letters were short and matter of fact, but as if in spite of himself some line appeared that was enough to bring hope and encouragement.

"Well, my Dear, here we are in the Whirl—Rather lonely some mornings, at breakfast in my room alone, but I like it in some ways. Bachelordom has its advantages! I miss Mother much in such big rooms and wish a certain young lady were only here to brighten them up with her smiles and silvery laugh; but she is having fine hours with many admirers no doubt."

If thoughts of marriage came to him then, he put them from his mind. His mother's health had begun to fail after her return from the coaching trip. She did not go back to Scotland with him for the summer, but preferred to stay at their cottage in Cresson Springs. Andrew joined her there in early autumn as soon as he returned from abroad.

In 1884 Charles Scribner published another of his books, called *Round the World,* this one taken from the notes he had written during the journey with Vandervort six years before. That year he made another coaching trip through Britain, taking British friends, writers and philosophers. He met William Gladstone, the Prime Minister, who had so impressed him when he first saw him at church with the Prince of Wales. A conversation with Gladstone gave him the idea for his third book.

"Do you know that a majority of the English-speaking race are republicans and the monarchists are in the minority?" he asked the Prime Minister.

"How's that?" Gladstone said in astonishment.

"There are more English-speaking people in the United States than in Great Britain and all her colonies," Carnegie went on.

"Ah! How's that? What is your population?"

"Sixty millions, and yours is not much more than half."

"Surprising!" the Prime Minister exclaimed.

Carnegie had other surprises in store for Gladstone, for he was filled with statistics about his adopted country. He pointed out that, according to the 1880 census, the hundred-year-old Republic could buy out all the realized capital and investments of Great Britain and Ireland, then pay off Britain's debt, and still her fortune would not be exhausted.

"America is now the largest manufacturing nation in the world," he went on. "Britain's manufactures in 1880 were worth 816 million pounds sterling. America's were worth 1,126 millions sterling."

"That's incredible!" Gladstone exclaimed. "Why doesn't some writer take up the subject and present it to the world?"

Andrew Carnegie had been gathering material on this subject since the results of the census of 1880 were published, and his mind was filled with statistics. The growth he had seen take place in his new country in the thirty-five years he had lived in it was unbelievable. In steel alone he had seen production jump from 64,000 tons in 1870 to 1,200,-000 in 1882, twelve years later.

When he first began to manufacture iron, he made a prediction that his company would soon produce more iron than the leading manufacturers of Scotland. This was soon after the Civil War, on one of his earlier visits to his native land. His host, one of the Scotch iron kings, had laughed at this boast, but fifteen years later the mills of America were producing not only more iron but also more steel than all of Great Britain combined. And his own company was the leading one. The rest of the world should know more about America's growth, and this was a story he wanted to tell. The notes he made after that were meant for a book that he would call *Triumphant Democracy,* but it could be written only in his spare time. "In a growing country like ours," he wrote, "a manufacturing concern begins to decay as soon as it stops expanding."

There was much the new country could learn from the old, however. In manufacturing iron and steel Carnegie saw, from the British companies, the need for owning the raw material. Though George Lauder's method of washing coke was a success, the supply was controlled by Henry Clay Frick. Soon after the Civil War, Frick, a former clerk in a dry-goods store, had begun buying small tracts of coke land. Like Carnegie, he saw the future of iron, and since coke was necessary for its production, he decided that was what he would acquire. During the panic of 1873 he was able to add to his vast holdings of land at a fraction of its value. At the age of thirty he was the largest coke producer in the world. Carnegie shrewdly saw that the Frick Coke Company not only had the best coal and coke property but also had, in Frick himself, the best man for its management. He went to Frick with an offer, and was able to buy half the shares in the company, adding to this with later purchases from other owners. Frick was then taken in as one of the ablest partners of his firm.

The chain of Carnegie's business interests had been developing link by link. Now there remained only one more link, and that was to own their supply of ironstone. A chemist was sent to examine the ores of various mines in search of the one with the least amount of phosphorus. He found it in an almost abandoned mine on the land of a wealthy farmer. Eighty shafts were sunk over a wide area, and the ore was analyzed at every few feet of depth, so the company would know exactly what there was of ironstone they were buying.

The Keystone Bridge Works were now building more bridges of steel than of iron. Since the invention of Thomas and Gilchrist, with the process of eliminating the phosphorus, the steel used for bridges and rails was purer than any made before. There were plans to build a new plant alongside the Edgar Thomson Mills, to make various shapes of steel, when Carnegie learned that the mills at Homestead, across the Monongahela River, could be bought. The new firm of Carnegie, Phipps and Company was organized to run the Homestead Mills, with Tom Carnegie at its head. The Hartman Steel Works at Beaver Falls was then established to manufacture articles from the steel produced at Homestead. Everything in steel, from a wire nail up to a twenty-inch steel girder, could be manufactured by the many plants owned by Carnegie and his associates.

While these firms were being organized and combined with the ones already established, Andrew Carnegie could not put the thought from his mind of the book he wanted to write about democracy in America. English lecturers had begun coming to this country, many in a critical mood, though knowing little about America. Even those who were sympathetic, such as Matthew Arnold and Herbert Spencer, both good friends of Carnegie, had little understanding of the tremendous growth of this Republic barely a hundred years old. "How little the best informed foreigner, or even Briton, knows of America, and how distorted that little is!" Carnegie said. It was to fill this need that *Triumphant Democracy* was written. He began it with a quotation from Emerson:

> God said I am tired of kings,
> I suffer them no more;
> Up to my ear the morning brings
> The outrage of the poor.
>
> And I will have never a noble,
> No lineage accounted great;
> Fishers and choppers and plowmen
> Shall constitute our state.

The American Republic, he wrote, had made little impression on the older lands until 1850, when the census showed her enormous gain in population and wealth. Ten years earlier she could claim no place among the principal nations, but every decade since then she had been overtaking them, one after the other.

The two earlier books had been a joy to write, compared to this one. Then he had looked forward to those rainy days when, free from thoughts of business, he could live again the summer's ride in coach-and-four, and the carefree months with Vandy in Japan, Singapore, India. With the book he was writing now, there were cold statistics to keep in mind, statistics on workmen's wages, on farm land, churches, schools, factories, railways. He wrote of prisoners, and of crime. America had not been backward in her treatment of prisoners, he wrote. Some states had even abolished the death penalty. Perhaps the next generation, or the next, would look back with horror on the punishment by death of human beings. He quoted Confucius, who, when asked by the king whether the unprincipled should not be killed for the sake of the principled, answered, "Sir, in carrying out your government, why should you kill at all?"

He proudly pointed out that in the United States, almost ten times as much money was spent for education as for armament. On the other hand, he said, in Great Britain alone, for every pound spent on education two and a half pounds were spent for armament.

"How long yet will men, instigated by royal and aristocratic jealousies spend their wealth and best energies upon means of slaughtering each other!"

For months Carnegie's head had been in a whirl of statistics, as well as of coke and iron ore and steel. There were times when he was scarcely aware whether it was noon or evening, so busy had he been, and so absorbed in what he was doing. The book was finished in 1886, the same year the Homestead Mills were established. He did not go to Scotland that summer, but stayed with his mother, now seventy-six and very feeble, in Cresson. The Alexander Kings had a summer home there, and he persuaded them to invite Mrs. Whitfield and her two daughters, Louise and Stella, for a few weeks. He was counting the days until their arrival, he said in a letter to Louise. Then he added, "Mother seems really better, it is miraculous. I trust yours is also better. Everything does hang upon our mothers, with both of us—our duty is the same, to stick to them to the last. I feel this every day."

By this time they were engaged, but there was no ring and no announcement was made. Mrs. Whitfield, though in poor health herself, was not one to stand in the way of her daughter's happiness. She was told of the engagement, but no one else was to know about it, not even Alexander and Aggie King, their closest friends. The courtship had not run smoothly. Two years earlier, Louise had sent back all the letters Andrew had written her, and asked for her own in return. There were hints that she would prefer marrying a poor man, one whom she could help rise in the world, as her mother had with her father. The years were passing, and she would soon be thirty. The correspondence began again soon afterward. A letter from Louise when he was in Scotland was promptly answered. When he returned, he had stopped overnight in New York before going down to Cresson to join his mother. He had walked past the Whitfield house and found it closed, with all the windows dark. The family had gone that summer to the Catskills. He wrote her, telling of his loneliness in looking up at the darkened windows and knowing she was gone. But he could not help mentioning his concern for his mother.

"I avoided the sad point till the last. Mother is not doing well. She was better for a few days, but this week there seems to be a relapse. She hasn't been out of bed for two days and I have the heart taken out of me whenever I fail to keep that subject out of my mind. Your letter this morning gave me a respite and I was bright and happy for a while. I hope you will write me now and then."

Louise's letters to him had a new tenderness that she no longer had to conceal. "I miss you so much, especially just now when I have so much to say to you which I cannot write, for my love lieth deep, too deep for swift telling."

The weeks spent at Cresson together were happy ones for both of them. Louise left with her mother and sister for New York, while Andrew stayed on at Cresson with his mother, with plans to meet Louise in the city later that winter. He had felt tired since finishing *Triumphant Democracy*. He thought it was due to strain and overwork in his business affairs and intense concentration on his writing. In October he took to his bed with a severe case of typhoid fever. He wrote to Louise about it, with a pencil on scratch paper. "Don't be alarmed," he said. "Nothing serious. Sure." Two days later he wrote again, saying, "I'll be very careful for a few days. Got your letter—the only one I've been allowed to get for three days."

His illness was far more serious than he had at first thought. He lay for six weeks under the care of an attendant physician and a trained nurse. His secretary sent telegraphic messages to Louise Whitfield from time to time, telling of his condition. In the meantime, his mother had had a relapse, and in the latter part of October his brother, Tom, was stricken with pneumonia and died within three days. Andrew was told nothing of this. He sensed something was wrong when he saw the doctor move quietly about his room once at midnight.

"What are you doing here so late?" Carnegie asked.

"Your mother needed me," the doctor replied, and it was not necessary to say more.

On his fiftieth birthday Andrew Carnegie lay hovering

between life and death. Gradually the pain and fever left his body, and a feeling of relaxation came over him. When he grew strong enough to bear the grief, he was told of the death of both his mother and his brother. From his window he could see the bare black trees, gnarled and twisted as if in agony, swaying against the background of the winter sky. Snow and ice silenced the earth, and it was as if all nature had died. He thought of his mother, his brother, and his father, whose lives had gone out at the time when the year drew near its end. It seemed only natural to him that he should follow his family in death. He lay in his bed, and waited.

Letters from Louise Whitfield, which he had been unable to see in his sickness, were given to him. He wrote to her, and there came over him hope and a strong desire to live. "Three months the doctor says I shall be better than for years and stronger. After that, Louise, the soul-hunger for your companionship must be satisfied. I'll run back to you and run away with you."

As soon as he could be safely moved, he was taken to the home of friends in New York, where he could regain his strength. Robert Pitcairn sent his private railway car for this purpose. One day a servant came in to announce a caller, Miss Louise Whitfield. They were married in April, and left at once for the Isle of Wight for their honeymoon. The wedding had been as quiet as the engagement, with only Louise's family present.

From the past year's depths of despair Andrew Carnegie now came to know the first real happiness of his life. And Louise, writing to her mother from London, said, "Truly my cup runneth over."

"Make that *our* cup runneth over," Andrew said when he saw what she had written.

They went to London for the Queen's Jubilee. Robert Browning called on them, as did Edwin Arnold, who had written *Light of Asia*. William Gladstone called, and invited them to dinner at his home. It was an informal visit, and while the ladies were visiting in another part of the house, Carnegie and Gladstone went to the library. Carnegie browsed over the shelves while Gladstone rearranged some of his books.

"Mr. Gladstone," Carnegie said, "I see a book written by a friend of my father's called *Dunfermline Worthies*. I knew some of those worthies as a child."

"Yes, and if you pass your hand three or four books to the left, I think, you will find another book by a Dunfermline man," the Prime Minister replied.

Carnegie looked, and to his surprise saw *An American Four-in-Hand in Britain*. Just then he heard the sonorous voice of the Prime Minister, from the top of the ladder, recite:

" 'What Mecca is to the Mohammedan, Benares to the Hindu, Jerusalem to the Christian, all that Dunfermline is to me.' "

"How on earth did you happen to have this book!" Carnegie exclaimed. "I didn't have the honor of knowing you when it was written, so I couldn't have sent you a copy."

"Someone told me about it, and I sent for it and read it with delight," Gladstone answered. "That tribute to Dunfermline struck me as so extraordinary, I can never forget it."

Uncle Lauder met them and took them to the house he

had found for them at Kilgraston, in Scotland. Nothing could have pleased Andrew Carnegie more than to discover that his wife shared his love of Scotland. He taught her to recognize the wildflowers that until then had been only names to her: Wandering Willie, heartsease, forget-me-nots, wild thyme. They went to Dunfermline, where anxious relatives were waiting to see whether she would accept them and become one of them, or whether she would come between them and their Andy. They had only to meet her to know their fears were groundless.

At Edinburgh, Carnegie was presented with the Freedom of the City, and his wife was beside him, sharing his honors. "A reception to Royalty was nothing compared to this," she wrote her mother. She was a little bewildered by the many visitors that filled the house at Kilgraston that summer. Matthew Arnold came; Blaine, the Secretary of State under Garfield, came with his wife and two daughters; Walter Damrosch, the young musician they had met on the boat coming over, was there as a house guest; Senator Hale and his wife, the Alexander Kings—the list of guests seemed endless. Often there were as many as eighteen at the table. With twenty servants, and a capable housekeeper who took over all the responsibility, Louise soon began to share her husband's delight in having friends around, though she wrote home that this big life was not altogether one she would choose. She added that Andrew was looking ten years younger, his complexion was clear, his eyes bright, and there was a happy look on his face. "I believe he becomes dearer to me every day of our lives."

Louise Carnegie was American to the core, and a Connecticut Yankee at that, her husband said. But she became as loyal a Scot as he. She wanted to go back every year. The following summer Carnegie rented Cluny Castle, not far from Edinburgh. Perhaps because Louise had not been able to go on his first coaching trip, with his triumphant entry into Dunfermline, he organized one for her this year. Lucy, Tom Carnegie's widow, gave them a splendid coach with British and American flags on the doors, and the seats covered with the tartan of the Carnegie clan. They started from London, Louise carrying a bouquet of roses and Carnegie wearing a red rose in his lapel. The Hales from Maine were with them, and also the Blaines. Because James G. Blaine's name had been mentioned for the coming presidential election, and he was much in the public eye, reporters followed the coach-and-four all during the journey, in dogcarts, buckboards, and on horseback.

They stayed for a night at Linlithgow Castle, the birthplace of Mary Queen of Scots. The town officials, dressed in their splendid robes of office, met them and paraded with them to the castle grounds. There were speeches of welcome and speeches of response. During the ceremonies a cable arrived with the news that the Republicans had nominated Benjamin Harrison as their candidate. James G. Blaine, for the second time, had lost his chance to become the country's President.

Cluny, the turreted castle of white granite, was owned by the head of the Macpherson clan. It was quiet and secluded, set in the midst of larches, fir, and birch, a thousand feet above the sea. As the coach approached the grounds, the coachman blew the horn to announce their arrival. This was answered by a salute of guns, and from the chimneys blue smoke rose up to meet the clouds. The cottagers waved to them as they passed, and Macpherson played his pipes as a greeting to them.

The summer was one long holiday. The June sun lingered in the sky, and the day drifted from twilight to dawn with scarcely a night between. Walter Damrosch, who was also one of the group, was the only one who needed candles as he played for them in the evening, and talked to them about the German composer Wagner. He had fallen in love with Margaret Blaine, and his own happiness was as great as that of the Carnegies. During the day they went fishing in Loch Laggan and hiked through the dark woods, crossing rustic bridges. They had picnics in the forest and tea parties in the summerhouse. The mountains surrounding their forest were treeless. During the summer they were covered with heather, and the rest of the year with snow. It was like the scenery in *Die Walküre,* they decided, and they pointed out where Brünnhilde was lying on a rocky summit surrounded by fire. The side of a brook was where Siegfried came upon the Rhinemaidens. Damrosch then burst into song, with passages of the music drama appropriate to the scene.

Louise took singing lessons from Damrosch that summer, so she could learn to sing the Scottish ballads that Andrew loved. When she first heard the Highland pipers, she declared that if she had to live on a lonely island and was allowed only one musical instrument, that would be the bagpipes. Her husband was so delighted with this remark that a piper was added to their household. He marched before them, playing them in to dinner, and in the mornings he paraded over the grounds outside the windows, piping them awake. On the Fourth of July he played "Yankee Doodle," which Damrosch had secretly taught him, to the surprise of his listeners.

Carnegie was interested in the young musician who was his guest. Damrosch had taken on the work of his father, who had died three years before. At twenty-seven he was director of the Oratorio Society, and conductor of the New York Symphony Orchestra. He had come to Europe the year before to study under the great pianist and conductor Hans von Bülow, and would return to New York that winter. With the enthusiasm of the young, he talked to Carnegie about his work and his dreams. The Metropolitan Opera House had been recently built, but the city needed a concert hall as well, one large enough for orchestral and choral music. Carnegie, encouraged by his wife, offered to give the building, but the people must support it. He had often said that he did not want to be remembered by what he gave, but by what he persuaded others to give. When a community was not ready to support the arts, it was not ready for the buildings to house them.

When he returned to New York that autumn, Carnegie formed an organization called the Music Hall Company of New York. Land was bought on the corner of Fifty-seventh Street and Seventh Avenue. The secretary of the Oratorio Society, William Burnet Tuthill, was chosen as the chief architect, and construction was begun. By the spring of 1891, Carnegie Hall was ready for its opening festival. Andrew and Louise Carnegie entered their rose-garlanded box, accompanied by the Blaines and their daughter Margaret, now Mrs. Walter Damrosch. They were applauded by the chorus of four hundred, already assembled on the stage.

Walter Damrosch came out and took his bow, then raised his baton to conduct. To him this was a fulfillment of his father's dream as well as his own. Music in America had come of age.

After the intermission, Tchaikovsky, the first great composer to visit this country, appeared on the stage to conduct his own works. He was greeted with a burst of applause.

After the concert Damrosch took him to meet the Carnegies. Lonely and homesick, the great composer felt immediately at home with the genial Scotsman.

"I was very much taken with the old man, especially as he is an admirer of Moscow, which he visited two years ago," Tchaikovsky wrote in his diary.

It surprised him to find that a man of such wealth could be so simple and unassuming. "Not in the least turning up his nose." Through Carnegie, Tchaikovsky became acquainted with the Scottish folksongs, which Damrosch played on a Steinway grand. Carnegie tried to persuade Tchaikovsky to come back to America the following year. He was in a gay mood that evening, and tried to cheer the melancholy Russian. He called him the uncrowned but true king of music. Standing on tiptoe, he raised his hands high to express the musician's greatness. Then, to the amusement of the other guests, he gave an imitation of the way Tchaikovsky had conducted. "He did it so well, so similarly, that I myself was delighted," the composer said.

Every summer for ten years the Carnegies returned to Cluny Castle, and came back in the autumn to their brownstone house on West Fifty-first Street in New York. In America they were publicly criticized for spending so much time in Scotland, when it was in this country that he made his money. Carnegie could not see any conflict in his love for Scotland and for America. The flags of both countries flew from his castle tower, and he felt an equal loyalty for each.

About the time plans for the concert hall had begun, Carnegie decided it was time to repay a debt to the city that had done so much for him. He offered to build a library in Pittsburgh, but the conditions were the same as with Carnegie Hall. The community must take up the responsibility of maintaining it.

"The main consideration should be to help those who will help themselves, to provide part of the means by which those who desire to rise, the aid by which they may rise; to assist, but rarely or never to do all. Neither the individual nor the race is improved by almsgiving," he wrote in an article for the *North American Review*.

In a letter to the mayor of Pittsburgh he made his offer of $250,000 for a library building, if the city would provide the site, and $15,000 a year for its support. This the city refused, but Allegheny City across the river, Carnegie's first American home, was glad to accept the same offer.

The building was finished a short while before the opening festival at Carnegie Hall, and Allegheny held a dedication ceremony for its new library and hall. President Harrison was the principal speaker.

He was the first United States President to visit this region, and his speech at Allegheny drew large crowds. The mayor and officials of Pittsburgh had reason to regret their refusal. Would Mr. Carnegie renew his offer? they asked. If so, the city would spend even more on maintenance than he had first suggested.

"No," Mr. Carnegie replied. "I'll quadruple my offer.

Would you accept a million dollars to use for a building?"

The offer was accepted without hesitation. A site was chosen, and a sufficient amount was decided upon for its maintenance. The library developed eventually into a group of buildings including a museum, an art gallery, and technical schools.

Before President Harrison left the city, he was shown the Carnegie steelworks, where the workmen gave him a cordial welcome. As they went from one department to another, Carnegie introduced the managers to him. He came to Charlie Schwab, the friendly, jovial young superintendent of the Homestead Mills.

"How is this, Mr. Carnegie? You present only boys to me," Harrison said.

"Yes, Mr. President, but do you notice what kind of boys they are?"

"Yes, hustlers. Every one of them."

Charlie Schwab, who once drove a mail coach and worked in a grocery store, started with the Edgar Thomson Mills as a stake driver. Before he was twenty he was made chief engineer and manager, and now, at twenty-eight, he was a partner, and well on his way to becoming a millionaire.

Andrew Carnegie seldom failed in his judgment of the men working under him. When he found one who impressed him with his intelligence, energy, and enthusiasm for the job, he put him in charge of the department he was best suited for, then left him alone with a free hand. Later these young managers were offered a partnership with the company at no expense to themselves. Their share was paid out of the profits.

Borntraegor, a partner and manager of the Lucy Furnaces, had started as a shipping clerk at six dollars a week. Abbot, also a partner and manager, had been an office boy. Curry, partner and manager of the Lucy Furnaces, had been a shipping clerk.

There was one who refused when a partnership was offered him. Captain Jones, who was largely responsible for the success of the Edgar Thomson Works, and whose name was famous wherever Bessemer steel was known, had started with the company as a two-dollar-a-day mechanic.

"Some of the young men who have been given an interest in the company are making more than you are, Captain Jones," Carnegie said one day. "We have voted to make you a partner, too."

He explained their policy of letting the profits pay for the cost of the shares, so there would be no financial responsibility. Captain Jones only shook his head. He had enough on his mind looking after the works, without taking on the worries of a partnership, he said. They could just give him a big salary if he was worth it.

"All right, Captain," Carnegie said with a laugh. "The salary of the President of the United States is yours."

Fifty thousand dollars a year!

"That's the talk!" the captain exclaimed.

Charles Schwab was promoted to the Edgar Thomson Works, and Henry Clay Frick was put in charge of the Homestead Mills. If there had been doubt about any of the partners, it would have been this one, who had not been chosen from the ranks. He had been valuable in making higher profits for the company, but he was ambitious to expand into other fields, forming a vast trust, as other industrialists were doing then. And to the workmen under him, he was cold and aloof, with little sympathy for their problems.

Andrew Carnegie was traveling in the Highlands of Scotland when a cable came telling of a strike at Homestead. It was two days late in reaching him, and he wired an answer at once, saying that he would take the next ship back. Another cable came urging him to remain where he was.

"We knew of his willingness always to grant the demands of labor, no matter how unreasonable," Henry Phipps said later.

Carnegie felt, with his partners, that the demands of the men were unreasonable. The company had installed new machinery costing millions of dollars, which enabled the men, paid by the tonnage, to earn 60 per cent more than before. He thought it fair that the men should have been content with a 30 per cent increase, and let the balance go toward paying for the improved equipment. If he had been at home, he would not have yielded to the demands of the men, he declared. Still, he would not have opposed a strike by them. His policy, which he had put down in writing, was that they should confer with the men, and wait patiently until the differences were settled and the workmen decided to return to work. Never would he hire new men to take the place of the strikers—never!

In Carnegie's absence Frick brought in strikebreakers. He hired a group of three hundred Pinkerton detectives, fully armed, to protect them. The strikers, led by a skilled mechanic named McLuckie, set out to drive away the strikebreakers and the detectives. This led to bloodshed, with seven guards and eleven strikers and spectators shot to death. The Governor of Pennsylvania sent in 8,000 troops to take charge of the situation.

"Nothing I have ever had to meet in all my life, before or since, wounded me so deeply," said Andrew Carnegie.

He cabled Phipps, urging him to have Charlie Schwab sent back to Homestead. This trouble would never have happened if he, instead of Frick, had been in charge. Schwab understood and liked the workmen, and he would be able to restore peace and harmony among them if anybody could.

When Carnegie returned to Pittsburgh that autumn, he found that suits had been entered against several of the strikers. He promptly had these dismissed. The mechanic McLuckie had been indicted for murder, riot, and treason, but he had made his escape, leaving all that he owned behind him. The company had won its battle, but not the sympathy of the people. It took a young anarchist, Alexander Berkman, to change that attitude. Two weeks after the strike Berkman walked into Frick's office, aimed a pistol at him, and fired. The attempt to assassinate Frick failed, but it was enough to shock the people, and for a long time they associated labor unions with anarchism.

In his talks with the men after they returned to work, Carnegie found them still resentful of the way Frick had acted.

"But you were badly advised," Carnegie said. "The offer was a generous one, and you should have accepted it. I don't know that I would have offered so much."

It wasn't a question of dollars, one of the rollers said. It was the man himself.

One of Andrew Carnegie's strongest traits was loyalty to

friends and associates. He was never heard to say anything against anyone, and he defended Frick when talking with others, but when the opportunity came, Frick was disposed of as a partner in the company. He had bought some land adjoining one of the plants, expecting the company to buy it for future expansion. He named a price of $150,000.

"What did you pay for it?" Carnegie asked him.

Frick refused to answer, saying it was his own personal affair. Carnegie investigated, and learned that he had paid only a third of the amount, and planned to make a profit of a hundred thousand dollars from his partners. Carnegie could not tolerate this kind of disloyalty.

He informed Frick that he was buying his interests and that he expected him to get out of the business. Frick refused to accept the terms of his offer, and held out for his own. Carnegie paid the price he demanded, but to his dying day Frick never forgave him.

A daughter was born to the Carnegies in March, 1897. After his first glimpse of her, her father said she was a little uncanny yet, fresh from heaven and not earthly like themselves. He had to be away from Louise for a while, and he wrote, "Oh Lou, may this be our last separation. I hope many, many long years together are to be ours with the little Darling closer and closer to us."

The child was named Margaret after her father's mother. When the news of her birth reached Cluny, the tenants lighted nine bonfires on the nine mountain peaks surrounding the castle. But there was to be another celebration at Cluny. The owner of the castle would be getting married soon, and he wanted the ancestral home for himself and his bride. Louise Carnegie had hoped to buy Cluny, for she

felt they should have a place of their own, in the Highlands
of Scotland, instead of a rented one that could be theirs
only at certain times. When they failed in their attempt to
buy Cluny, Carnegie began inquiring about other places
that might be bought. When he returned to Scotland he was
driven in a wagonette over an old road that led to Skibo
Castle, once the Bishop's Manor, which stood overlooking
the Firth of Dornoch in northern Scotland. Everything about
the place was going to decay. The roads were unkept; the
farms were in poor condition; the houses of tenants and
workers in need of repair. But there was a wild beauty about
the place. The estate ran from the shores of Dornoch Firth
for miles to the western border, and it had the same quiet
serenity they had found at Cluny. Carnegie rented the place
for a year with an option to buy. In May of 1898 he, Louise,
and little Margaret, with all their household servants, moved
to Skibo. All the villages on the estate were decorated with
flags and bunting, and the children, dressed in their Sunday
best, had been let out of school for the occasion. Bagpipes
played a greeting to them, and the oldest tenant, a man almost ninety, gave the address of welcome to the new Laird
of Skibo.

# CHAPTER XII "A Web Begun"

The year 1900 gave promise of a new era. The Century of Hope, it was called. In books and magazine articles there were prophecies about what the new century would bring. Wealth would be shared. There would be equality for all, and an end to want. Nations would learn to live in peace with one another, and wars would be unheard of. Still the war dragged on in South Africa between the British and the Dutch, and China was besieged by European troops, and even some from America. In the second year of the century President McKinley was killed by the anarchist Leon Czolgosz. For the third time within thirty-six years, a President of the United States was assassinated.

In March of 1901 Andrew Carnegie decided the time had come to keep the promise he had made to himself. He would give up accumulating money and begin distributing it for the two causes closest to his heart, education for the young, and peace among nations.

J. P. Morgan approached him through Charlie Schwab, with the word that if Mr. Carnegie really meant to sell his business and retire, he thought it could be arranged. Carnegie set his price at $300,000,000, which Morgan accepted without hesitation. Since the amount did not include the value of the common stock, then steadily earning 5 per cent, Carnegie later learned that he could have asked a hundred million more and Morgan would have paid it as willingly. There were rumors on Wall Street of how this rankled in his soul, but it was denied by Carnegie himself. He had considered what he felt was a fair price, he said, and Charlie Schwab arranged the sale for this amount at his bidding. As it was, the sale had made him the richest man in America. Andrew Carnegie had been canny. No one had been able to get the better of him in the business world, though many had tried. But he could take satisfaction in knowing that this money had been earned through work and good management, and not by manipulating the stock market, gambling with other people's money, or by bringing prices down and forcing out competitors, as many fortunes were made.

He was sixty-five at that time, still active and alert. A feeling of emptiness came over him when he walked out of his office, never to return. For more than a half century, since his first job in the cotton mill as bobbin boy, he had had the responsibility of work, and he would miss it. He knew he would be tempted many times to go back to the mills just to see how things were going, but he would force himself to stay away.

The day after the sale, on the twelfth of March, he made a gift to the workmen, whose labor, he said, had contributed so much to his success. A fund of $4,000,000 was established to provide pensions for those needing help in old age, and for the relief of any who suffered from accidents. Another $1,000,000 was given to maintain the libraries and lecture halls he had built for them earlier.

Soon after this, he sailed for Europe and Skibo with his wife and daughter, now four years old. Some of the former partners, "the boys," his wife called them, came to the ship to see him off. It was a sad parting for Carnegie, a farewell to an integral part of his life.

Though Skibo had been remodeled, with Pittsburgh steel, electricity, plumbing, and elevators, its towers and parapets still held all its ancient charm. Large windows looked out over moor and meadow, and from one of the towers a flag was raised, showing on one side the Union Jack and on the other the Stars and Stripes.

All five little villages on the estate had been restored, and now looked neat and well kept, each with its school and library. On the closing day of school the Carnegies had a festival for the children, with speeches and prizes and hampers of cake and sandwiches and lemonade.

The grounds were so large and the scenery so varied that while Carnegie went trout fishing at a wild moorland lake surrounded by heather, Louise took Margaret down to a beach where the child could play barefoot in the sand, with blue waves rolling in at her feet. A mountain stream went tumbling through a wild ravine on its way to the firth. When it came to a narrow pass, it fell headlong, churning and foaming, into a rocky pool. Here the salmon came once a year for their long, arduous journey upstream to spawn. The Carnegies and their guests stood watching them leap and fall back, time and again, never giving up until one mighty leap took them up to the higher level where they could swim on to fresh water.

In the evening after supper the Carnegie family and their guests gathered in the drawing room beside a roaring fire. An organist played Bach or Haydn during the week, and hymns on Sundays. When the music ended, Carnegie, in his wavery tenor voice, sang the Scottish songs his father used to sing, or he recited scenes from *Macbeth* or *King Lear*.

"What a sane and happy home it is. One forgets it is a castle," one of the guests wrote after a visit there.

King Edward made a surprise, informal visit to Skibo. Buckingham Palace was being remodeled at that time, and he was interested in Skibo's modern conveniences. Margaret came into the room with flowers she had been gathering in the garden and presented them to the king, who only smiled indulgently when she forgot to make her curtsy.

In the summer of his retirement, Andrew Carnegie thought of an article he had read four years earlier, written by Thomas Shaw, a Dunfermline friend, about education in Scotland. A primary and a secondary education were within the reach of all, but only the sons and daughters of the rich could go beyond this, to a college or university. The idea came to him to establish a fund of $10,000,000, half of the income to be used to provide scholarships to those who could not afford a higher education, and the other half to improve the universities.

This was only a small beginning. He could see now the tremendous task facing him in distributing his wealth. His millions were bringing in an income of several more millions a year, adding that much to the money to be given away. He returned to New York with his family in the fall. Something he read in a paper impressed him. "The gods send thread for a web to weave." It seemed a message meant especially for him. He would begin his web at once. The gods sent their thread through a suggestion from the director of the New York Public Libraries, and a pattern was formed. Five and a quarter million dollars went to build sixty-eight branch libraries in New York City, and twenty more libraries were built in Brooklyn. Carnegie chose capable advisers with the same care with which he had chosen partners in his business, and left much of the administration to them.

The Carnegies lived simply in comparison to other wealthy people. The house on West Fifty-first Street, where they lived for the first fifteen years of their marriage, was a brownstone very much like the others on the block. In the year he bought Skibo, Carnegie bought some land in New York for a new home. This was on Fifth Avenue between Ninety-first and Ninety-second streets, considered at that time far uptown and away from the fashionable neighborhood. In the autumn of 1902, when they returned from their summer in Scotland, the Carnegies moved into their new home. They drove from the landing pier, through Central Park, followed by reporters all the way. The familiar faces of the household staff were there to greet them, and as they passed through the doorway an organist played favorite selections from Handel.

It was the home of a very rich man, but a man who loved books, music, and the company of congenial friends, and who cared nothing for display. There were fifty large rooms, including a ballroom, a drawing room with panelled walls of red brocade, a dining hall large enough for as many guests as they wanted to entertain. A large picture gallery was at the east end of the house, and at the west there was a stately library where formal conferences could be held. Over the wide fireplace of the library a motto was carved, "The Hearth Our Altar, Its Flame Our Sacred Fire." Carnegie's favorite books were kept in a smaller room, which he called his working library. His own bedroom was simple, as were rooms he had known as a child. The only wall decoration was a painting of Captain Bill Jones, who had been killed in an accident at the Edgar Thomson Works in 1889. In a fast-growing city of brick and stone, it was unusual to find a garden, but here there were flower beds and a lawn, and a summerhouse open to the breeze.

The first dinner party given at the new house was for the former business partners, forty-seven in all. They called themselves the Carnegie Veterans' Association, though to Mrs. Carnegie they were still "the boys." They made a vow to meet every year, and never to disband until the last member died.

Another annual dinner was for their literary friends, such as Mark Twain, Henry James, John Burroughs, Josh Billings, President Eliot of Harvard. "The chief glory of a nation is its authors" were the words carved on the frieze of the library mantel. At the first dinner the guests were asked to write their names on the tablecloth. This was later embroidered, and the signatures served as place cards for the annual dinners afterward. "Knights of the Cloth" they were called.

Members of the Oratorio Society were dinner guests from time to time. Famous statesmen, American and foreign, visited the Carnegies. There were also college professors, newspaper editors, scientists, and others whose lives were spent in benefiting mankind. Andrew Carnegie was always the genial host, ready to listen, and ready to enliven the conversation. Even when alone, walking in his garden behind the iron rail fence, he enjoyed talking with any passer-by who stopped to admire the flowers.

The industrialism that had defeated his father had given him vast wealth. Now his wealth was being used to repay the debt industrialism owed to the world: $60,000,000 of the Carnegie money went to build 2,800 libraries in this country and Britain; and $24,000,000 more were spent for the people of Pittsburgh on the Carnegie Institute with an art gallery, a museum of the natural sciences, and a concert hall. Through such gifts as these, the Carnegie Institute of Technology and the Carnegie Library of Pittsburgh, Andrew Carnegie was able to give back to his adopted city some of the wealth it had bestowed upon him. For the nation's Capital he established the Carnegie Institution of Washington, for scientific research. He began to see the far-reaching results of his gifts, in the work they were doing. The Institution built an observatory on Mount Wilson in California, with lenses more powerful than any at that time. A hundred new stars were discovered, some twenty times the size of the sun.

"All we know is as nothing to the unknown," Carnegie said.

The twentieth century saw men going off to the last unexplored regions of the earth. After many heartbreaking attempts, Admiral Peary reached the North Pole, and two years later the South Pole was discovered by the Norwegian Captain Amundsen. Wilbur and Orville Wright made a successful flight in a heavier-than-air machine, and the age-old dream of man to fly was realized. A plane flew across the English Channel at almost a mile a minute, and the first nonstop flight from Albany to New York, of 137 miles, was made in 152 minutes. The horseless carriage was no longer an experiment, a rich man's toy, when Henry Ford began manufacturing automobiles within the reach of the workingman.

With distances made shorter by speed, and the last of the unexplored places known and charted, the need was greater than ever for nations to live in peace. Andrew Carnegie looked upon his Hero Fund as his first effort to bring this about. "My ain bairn" he called the idea, for it came to him without any suggestion or advice from others. Men who killed or maimed their fellow men on the battlefield were heroes of barbarism, he said. The hero of civilization was the man who risked or gave his life to save another. To the French people he said that their real hero was Pasteur, not Napoleon.

Funds were established in America and nine European countries so that these heroes and their dependents or survivors could be recognized and honored. The medal given then had more meaning than a military decoration. With it went some needed reward, such as establishing one in business, giving another money to pay off his debts or to buy a home or pay for his education. Disabled heroes or dependents of those who died while performing a heroic act were given benefits according to their need.

In 1910 the Carnegie Endowment for International Peace was established, with a gift of $10,000,000. Carnegie wrote to the trustees he had chosen that the revenue of this was to be administered to hasten the abolition of international war, which he called the foulest blot upon our civilization:

> Although we can no longer eat our fellow men nor torture prisoners, nor sack cities, killing their inhabitants, we

still kill each other in war like barbarians. Only wild beasts
are excusable for doing that in this, the twentieth century
of our Christian era, for the crime of war is inherent, since
it decides not in favor of right, but always of the strong.
The nation is criminal which refuses arbitration and drives
its adversary to a tribunal which knows nothing of righteous
judgement. . . .

He had full confidence in the trustees, he said, leaving to
them the widest discretion as to what policy they should
adopt, only to bear in mind the one end they should keep
in view: the speedy abolition of international war. When
this was accomplished, and war was discarded, as dueling
and slavery had been discarded, the trustees would consider
what was the next most degrading evil to be banished, and
what could be done that would most advance the progress,
elevation, and happiness of man, and so on from century to
century without end.

The witnesses to this letter were his wife, who had been a
partner in all his giving, and his daughter, Margaret, a quiet,
unspoiled girl of thirteen.

For ten years Andrew Carnegie devoted himself tirelessly
to the task of distributing his wealth. With still $150,000,-
000 left, he set aside a tenth of this for himself and his
family; then he organized the Carnegie Corporation, with
a board of trustees of his choosing, to continue carrying out
his plan of giving, even after his death. To be held in trust
were $135,000,000, with the income used for advancing
and spreading knowledge.

"A man should not only have something to retire with,
but he should have something to retire to," he said.

He built a lodge of gray stone on the grounds of Skibo,

several miles away from the castle. Here he and Louise and Margaret went every July, to find solitude. They took only the necessary servants, but no valet, no personal maid, no secretaries. Carnegie still enjoyed writing letters to the editors of newspapers, expressing his views on various subjects. He also wrote his own life story, picking up his writing pad from time to time, to scribble a few paragraphs with a lead pencil. He wrote of his early years, of the poverty and struggle, and of the long climb from want to undreamed-of wealth. He read old letters from friends and relatives long gone.

As he sat in his favorite chair with the pad on his knee, writing and reliving the past, Louise was beside him, writing to friends or jotting the happenings of the day in the journal she had kept from her childhood. She could smile now with contentment, as she looked back on the pages she had written in the days of their courtship. "Had delightful horseback ride with Mr. Carnegie," to be followed by, "Am so unhappy, so miserable." Again, "Am so happy tonight. Mr. Carnegie came and spent afternoon with me." One New Year's Eve she had written, "And now we come to the last night of the old year again. What a changed girl this finds me! I feel so old and strange. Nothing is certain, nothing is sure."

Carnegie wrote only briefly of their courtship in his autobiography. But now, after twenty years of marriage, he could write of his happiness with her. He quoted Ferdinand's words to Miranda from Shakespeare's *The Tempest:*

> Full many a lady
> I have eyed with best regard . . . for several virtues
> Have I liked several women; never any

With so full soul, but some defect in her
Did quarrel with the noblest grace she owed
And put it to the foil: but you, O you,
So perfect and so peerless, are created
Of every creature's best.

"In my soul I could echo these very words. Today, after twenty years of life with her, if I could find stronger words I could truthfully use them," he added. He could not imagine himself going through those twenty years without her. Nor could he endure the thought of living without her. In the course of nature, he would be spared that. He would be the first to go, but at the thought of death, he wrote, "Why, oh, why are we compelled to leave the heaven we have found on earth and go we know not where!"

The horseback rides they had once enjoyed had now given way to quiet strolls together, at Skibo along the paths they called the Monks' Walk, or the Sunset Walk, and in New York they went every fair day to Central Park and walked around the Reservoir.

Every mail brought letters by the hundreds, with requests for money. No one person could read them all, but as many as possible were brought to Carnegie's personal attention. He spent several hours a day at the desk in his working library, going over them. The operator who had taught him telegraphy was old and in want. A yearly income was given him from the pension fund Carnegie had set up in the year of his retirement. Pensions were given to the men who had worked for him when he was with the Pennsylvania Railroad. The telegraphers with him during the Civil War were not eligible for government pensions, so they too, or their widows, received pensions from him. An old woman who had rocked him in his cradle in Dunfermline, some of his former schoolmates, all who had ever shown him kindness, were remembered. These pensions he gave often made the difference between a contented old age and one of misery. He thought of Robert Barryman, the sailor, who had bought the cool drink of sarsaparilla for a bewildered immigrant boy. For years he had tried to trace him, but no one knew what had happened to him. He learned that McLuckie, the skilled mechanic who had led the strikers at Homestead, had been found, alone and penniless, in Mexico. He made arrangements to have money sent to him anonymously. When McLuckie found a good job and was able to refuse help, he was told that the offer had come from Andrew Carnegie, whom he had thought his enemy.

A pension fund was established for university professors, to dignify and encourage the profession of the teacher. On the meager salaries they were paid, Carnegie felt that it was impossible for them to save for their old age. Writers also were given financial help if they were in need. Such people were performing a service to mankind, and should not be burdened with anxiety about earning a living, he said.

"You can take my halo," Mark Twain wrote him when he heard about it.

In looking back over his gifts, large and small, with their far-reaching results, Andrew Carnegie thought of the one closest to his heart, and wrote about it in his journal. "No gift I have ever made, or can ever make, can possibly approach that of Pittencrieff Glen."

Pittencrieff Glen, that paradise of his childhood he had been forbidden to enter, how many generations of children had tried to steal a glimpse of it through the gates or over the wall! When Carnegie learned that the present Lord Hunt would sell it for a little over $200,000, he cabled his friend and agent in Scotland to buy it for him. On Christmas Eve a cable came in reply, "Hail, Laird of Pittencrieff!"

"The King," Carnegie wrote, "well, he is only a king. Poor man, he doesn't own King Malcolm's tower, nor St. Margaret's shrine, nor Pittencrieff Glen."

The grandson of Thomas Morrison, and nephew of the rebel Bailie Morrison, opened wide the gates of Pittencrieff Glen to everyone. It was made into a recreation park with an endowment for its upkeep. "Not for a crown would I barter that privilege," Carnegie declared.

The ruins of King Malcolm's tower he kept for himself, and with it the memory of his father singing as he wove his web:

> The king sits in Dunfermline tower,
> Drinking the blude-red wine.
> "O whar will I find a good sailor
> To sail this ship o' mine?"

The abolition of war was still uppermost in Andrew Carnegie's mind. In 1913 he went to the dedication of the Peace Palace at The Hague, his gift to the Netherlands government. He was then seventy-eight, and felt he was nearing the end of his life. "The day that International Court is established will become the most memorable day in the world's history," he wrote. "It will ring the knell of man killing man—the deepest and blackest of crimes."

People came from all over the world for the dedication ceremonies at The Hague. There were turbaned Indians and Turks with red fezzes, Chinese in coats of silk brocade and

Japanese in dark kimonos. All had come in a desire for peace. Inside the stately hall the Queen of the Netherlands sat on a dais under a canopy of crimson velvet embroidered in gold. The light shone softly on the hangings of Oriental prayer rugs along the walls. Outside, the sun was shining gloriously and all the bells were ringing. The streets were thronged, and in the hearts of the people there was hope.

Less than a year later the heir to the Austrian throne, Archduke Francis Ferdinand and his wife, were assassinated in Serbia, and soon the whole world was plunged into war. Andrew Carnegie wrote the last entry in his journal: "The world is convulsed by war as never before! Men slaying each other like wild beasts. I dare not relinquish all hope—" His hope was in Woodrow Wilson, who might, he said, become the immortal leader the world needed. This could be a war to end wars. "Nothing is impossible to genius! Watch President Wilson! He has Scotch blood in his veins." Here he put down his pen and wrote no more about his life.

President Wilson was re-elected under the slogan "He kept us out of war!" In March, 1917, the month of his inauguration, the United States declared war against Germany, and three months later the first American troops landed in France.

The war made it impossible for the Carnegies to spend their summers at Skibo. Louise Carnegie searched for a country home in the Berkshires. She found what she wanted in Shadowbrook, an estate of six hundred acres formerly owned by Anson Phelps Stokes. The house was built on a hill that sloped down to Lake Mahkeenac. It had the quiet seclusion they had found at Cluny and at Skibo, with a view of green hills and blue water that had stretched for miles around. Mrs. Carnegie first saw the place in the setting sun, and she said that life there could be an Americanized Skibo. The piper was with them there, as he had been at Skibo. It was a strange sight on the American landscape to see him, his bonnet cocked on one side of his head, his kilt swishing with every step as he strode proudly over the grounds, piping the Carnegie clan tune to waken the household in the morning. There was an organist there too, as at their New York home and at Skibo.

Germany surrendered in 1918. The Kaiser abdicated and fled to Holland. On November 11th the armistice was declared, and the war came to an end. The war to end wars, the people called it, and again there was hope for a world of peace.

Andrew Carnegie was then eighty-three. For the past two years he had been failing in health. He spent his days quietly, the summers at Shadowbrook and winters at his home in New York, listening by the hour to the music played by his organist, or sitting in a steamer chair in the garden, with a nurse in attendance. Sometimes his thoughts went back to the past, as an old man's will, to the dreams of his childhood and how they had come true beyond his expectations. The little boy drawing water at the public well, wishing for the time when his parents could ride in a carriage of their own, had become the friend of kings and presidents. King Edward, in appreciation for all he had done for Great Britain, wanted to bestow some honor upon him, but Andrew Carnegie would have no title of nobility. A letter from the king was all he wanted, and this letter he still had in his possession.

In his desk was a box filled with things he had treasured

from childhood, mementos of his father and mother, an old Bible, a little packet of documents on which he had written "Cannot destroy." One of the documents was the original mortgage on the house on Rebecca Street, signed in his mother's trembling hand. On the back was a record of payments of $100 each, with the final discharge in April, 1856. There was also a box in his desk, containing an old-fashioned red leather pocketbook. Inside it was a sheet of paper on which, a half century ago, he had written his resolution to give up amassing wealth when he had enough, and to begin disposing of it for benevolent purposes. It had taken him much longer than the two years he had then allowed himself, but he had lived up to it.

Margaret Carnegie was married in the spring of 1919, on the thirty-third anniversary of her parents' wedding. Her husband, Roswell Miller, was the son of an old family friend. The bagpipes, with streamers fluttering gaily, were played at the wedding, and Carnegie danced briefly with his daughter.

Dod came for a visit that summer, and Andrew Carnegie felt well enough to go fishing at Shadowbrook. Death came quietly on the eleventh of August. Andrew Carnegie had paid his debt to the world for the good life given him. Words he had written earlier were now remembered:

"It would be no greater miracle to be born to a future life than to have been born to live in this present life. The one has been created, why not the other? Therefore there is reason to hope for immortality. Let us hope."

# Index

213